Miscalculation: Risks of Inadvertent Nuclear War

SAGHIR IQBAL

ISBN-10: 1717040403
ISBN-13: 978-1717040404

DEDICATION

I dedicate this book to all those who gave me encouragement, support and guidance. Foremost, to my father (late) Raja Mohammed Iqbal and to my mother Azra Begum, from whom I have learnt so much. In addition, to my great grandfather (late) Raja Abbas Ali Khan, my grandfather (late) Khan Mohammed Khan and Raja Adalat Khan. Raja Shah Mohammed Khan (late, grandfather maternal side), Raja Feroze Khan (late) , Raja Sher Mohammed Khan (late), Sandal Begum (late, grandmother maternal side), Also to my father-in-law (late) Raja Alf Khan, My uncles (maternal side) (late) Raja Mohammed Ashrif and (late) Raja Mohammed Aslam, to my uncles, paternal side (late) Raja Baaz Khan, (late) Raja Mohammed Rauf (General) and (late) Raja Naseer Ahmed, Raja Bashir Ahmed, Raja Qurban Khan, Raja Ajaib Khan, Raja Zareef Khan, Raja Saghir Khan.

Also dedicated to Raja (Major) Muhammed Ayub Iqbal, Raja Tariq Iqbal, Raja Tika Iqbal, Raja Waheed Iqbal, Raja Asif Iqbal, Raja Sufyan Ahmed, Raja Suleiman Ahmed, Raja Shokot Ali and to Kauser Ali. Furthermore, Raja Allahdad Khan, Raja Mohammed Yasin, Raja Khizer Iqbal, Raja Adil Khan, Raja Adnan Khan, Raja Zahid Khan, Raja Naser Khan, Raja Qasim Khan, Sarda Begum and (late) Zarda Begum.

And finally, to Raja Asghar Ali, Raja Imran Khan, Raja Kamran Khan, Raja Sohail Tariq, Raja Usama Tahir, Raja Khurram Iqbal, Raja Mohammad Uzaire Ali, Husnaa Tahir, Sanha Khan, Fareeda Khan, Qundeel Tariq, Umera Tariq, Raja Aadam Tahir, Raja Yusuf Tahir and Zainab Iqbal for their constant support and help.

CONTENTS

ACKNOWLEDGMENTS

I am very grateful to a host of people for their various contributions towards this book. I am particularly very grateful to Professor Syed Peerzada Mahmud Shah Bookhari who deserves much commendation for his constant encouragement and support throughout the hard times of the programme. I am also very grateful for Husnaa Tahir for her work and support in making this book a reality.

Miscalculation: Risks of Inadvertent Nuclear War

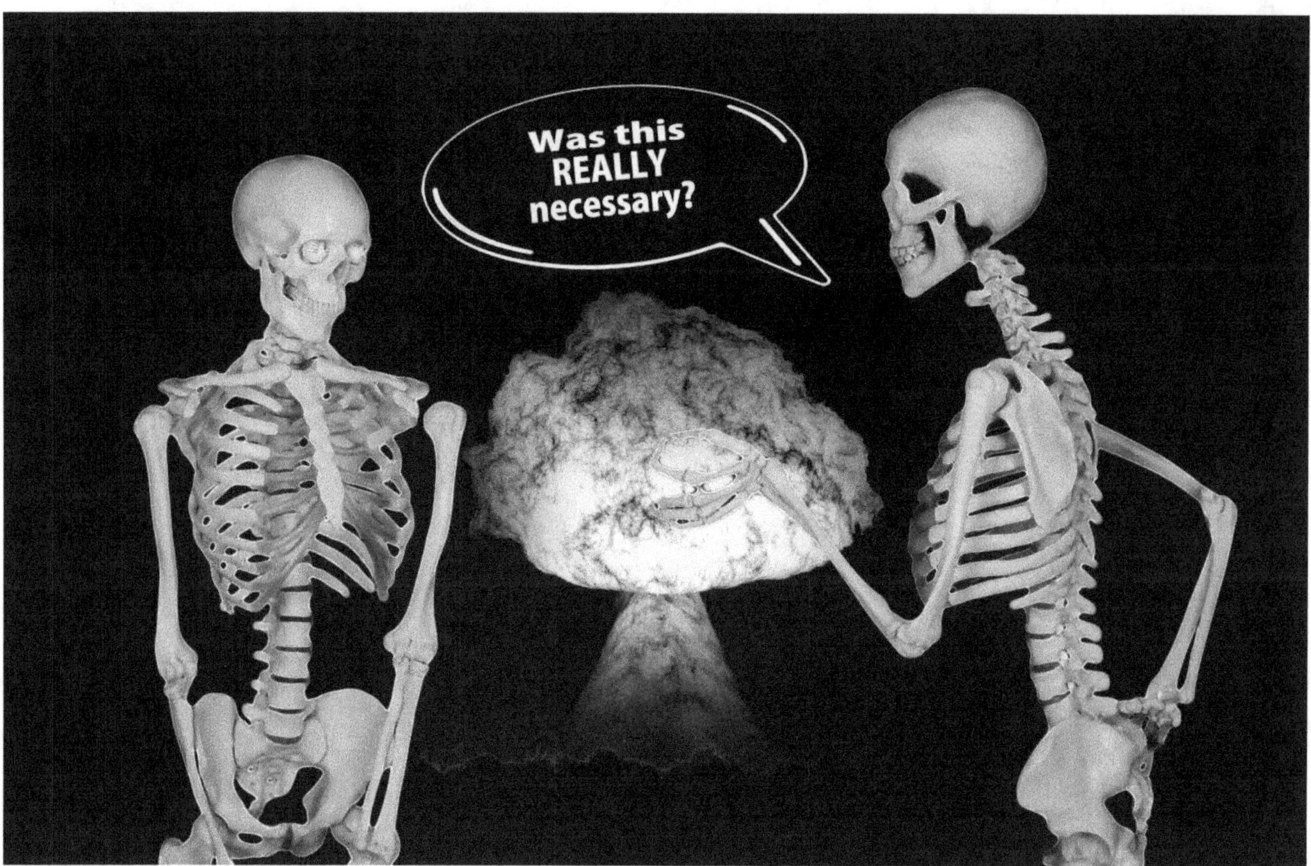

Abstract

The simmering Kashmir dispute between India and Pakistan has resulted in a nuclear arms race between these two powers. Pakistan's relations with India are marked by mutual distrust, divergence in foreign policy goals, and period tension. The current bitterness between Pakistan and India can be ascribed to a number of events. They include India's desire to play a dominant role in South Asia and its efforts to put down the nationalist struggle in in Indian occupied Kashmir, the conventional and nuclear arms race, and charges of interference in each other's internal affairs

From the early 1980s until now, the uprising in Kashmir again brought the armies of Pakistan and India very close to conflict. Tensions have continued due to the heavy handed and brutal tactics that India has done to the Kashmiri people in Indian occupied Kashmir. The Kashmiri separatist/freedom fighter, Burhan Wani's death on July 9, 2016 has sparked mass protests, with over 50,000 people congregated to mourn his death and joined his funeral procession. With Indian development of Cold Start Doctrine (CSD) and a hawkish Hindu Fundamentalist government (BJP) — serious border firing has led to extreme tensions, which has the potential to breakout into an all-out war with nuclear Pakistan. The Kashmir dispute is deemed to be the world's most dangerous issue, which has the highest chance of a catastrophic inadvertent nuclear war occurring between India and Pakistan.

AH-64D Apache attack helicopter (India has ordered this sophisticated US attack helicopter)

Abbreviation

AAM – Air-to-air missile

AAR - Air to air refuelling

APC – Armoured Personal Carrier

AEW&C – Airborne Early Warning and Control Aircraft

ALCM/GLCM – Air Launched Cruise Missile/ Ground Launched Cruise Missile

AWACS – Airborne Warning and Control System

BMD – Ballistic Missile Defence

BVR – Beyond Visual Range (air-air-missile)

CSD – Cold Start Doctrine

ICBM – Intercontinental Ballistic Missile

IAF – Indian Air Force

JF-17 – Joint Fighter 17 Thunder (Pakistani derivative)

MBT – Main Battle Tank

MIRV – Multiple Independently Targetable Reentry Vehicle

NCWF – New Concept of War Fighting

PAF – Pakistan Air Force

PN – Pakistan Navy

PGM - Precision guided munitions (Smart weapons)

SAM – Surface to Air Missile

SLCM – Submarine Launched Cruise Missile

SLBM – Submarine Launched Ballistic Missile

UCAV – Unmanned Combat Aerial Vehicle

F-16 Fighting Falcon

Chapter 1: Kashmir – Disputed Territory

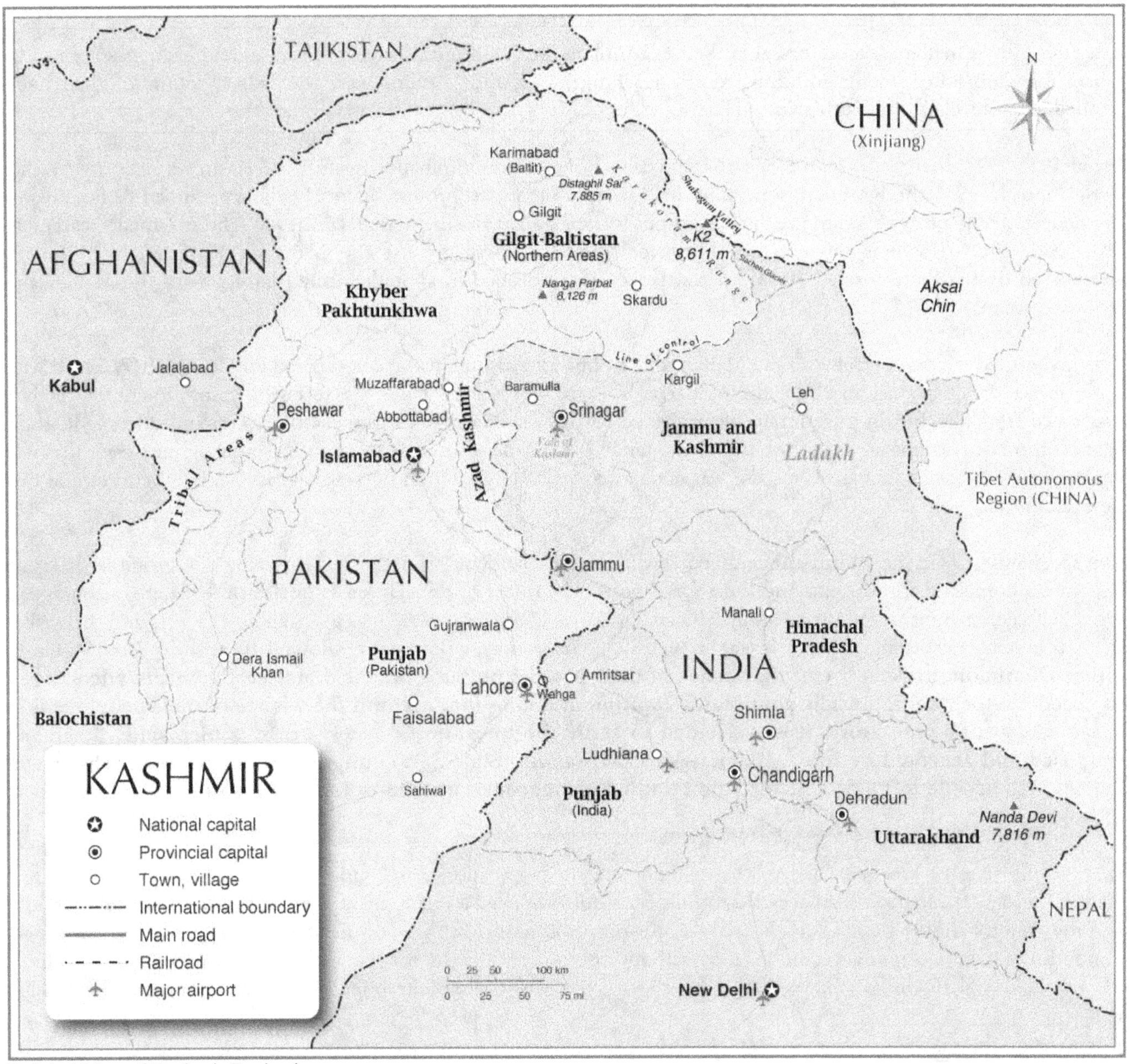

Political Map of Kashmir Region[1]

Kashmir: history of a flashpoint

The bone of contention between India and Pakistan is the province of Kashmir. Both sides put a claim to it, since they both received independence from British India. Historically, Kashmir was sold in 1846 (including its population) by the British East India Co (colonial rulers of India) to a Hindu Maharajah for six million rupees and an annual tribute of six shawls spun from the wool of Kashmiri goats.[2] The Kashmiri Muslim population, saw the British illegally empowering Hari Singh to rule over a majority Muslim state.

---

[1] Political Map of the Kashmir Region - http://www.nationsonline.org/oneworld/map/Kashmir-political-map.htm

[2] Lars Eriksen, Kashmir: history of a flashpoint (2002)- https://www.theguardian.com/world/2002/jun/09/india.kashmir3

In the past, Kashmir was ruled by four Hindu maharajas that ruled for a span of 100 years, namely Gulab, Ranbir, Pratap and Hari Singh, they were ruling over a predominantly Muslim state (after capturing the Kashmiri state from its previous Muslim rulers). Kashmir was initially controlled by the Muslim Durrani Empire of Afghanistan, and four centuries of Muslim rule under the Mughals and the Afghans in 1819.[3]

The four Hindu maharajas were brutal in their in handling the Kashmiri Muslim population and each was seen to be worse than the other. In the Muslim majority Kashmiri state, the Muslims were the worst victims of their high-handedness, especially the last Maharaja Hari Singh.[4]

From 1925-1947, Maharajah Hari Singh continued his policy of discrimination against the Kashmiri majority Muslim population. In 1931 the Kashmiri population held its first organised protest against his heavy handed tactics against the people. These protests led to the 'Quit Kashmir' campaign against the Maharaja in 1946 (and eventually leading to the Azad (Free) Kashmir movement).[5] However, the movement against the Maharaja Hari Singh is brutally suppressed by the State forces.[6] Kashmiri resistance are embroiled in sporadic armed battles with the Maharajah's troops in August 1947.

The first armed encounter between the Maharajah's troops and insurgent forces occurred in August 1947. Faced with a Kashmiri revolt against his rule, the Maharaja flees to Jammu in which he received commitment of military assistance from the Indian government in exchange for his signing the 'Instrument of Accession' document. India gains control of Kashmir in return for armed assistance. This leads to Indian troops in Kashmir fighting their first war against Pakistan. On 1 January 1949, the war ends after a UN intervention puts up a ceasefire line between the two new nations.[7]

On 15 August 1947, the Indian subcontinent becomes independent – on the basis of religious grounds, Pakistan becomes a homeland for Muslims and India for Hindus. The rulers of princely states in British India are encourage to move with either India or Pakistan Kashmir by taking into account factors such as geographical factors and the wishes of their people. Accordingly (Peace Kashmir Website), **"In theory, rulers were allowed to accede their States to either Dominion, irrespective of the wishes of their people; but as a practical matter, they were encouraged to accede to the geographically contiguous Dominion, taking into account the wishes of their people and in cases where a dispute arose, it was decided to settle the question of accession by a plebiscite, a scheme proposed and accepted by India. Being a Muslim majority State and contiguous to Pakistan, Kashmir was expected to accede to Pakistan; since the Hindu Ruler acceded instead to India, a dispute arose in the case of Kashmir"**.[8]

In 1948 the state of Junagadh had a Muslim Ruler but the population was Hindu majority. The Muslim Ruler had wanted to Join Pakistan and had acceded to this. But India imposed a plebiscite in the state for the people to choose and the Hindu majority population chose India. Kashmir was a mirror image of the state of Junagadh, but this time a Hindu Ruler over Kashmir acceding to India without offering a plebiscite for the Muslim majority population – India did not hold a plebiscite as it knew that the wishes of the Muslim majority population was to join up with Muslim Pakistan.[9]

---

[3] Schofield, Victoria (2010), Kashmir in conflict: India, Pakistan and the unending war, I. B. Tauris.

[4] The Hindu maharajas of Kashmir - https://www.pakistantoday.com.pk/2016/04/24/the-hindu-maharajas-of-kashmir/

[5] History of Kashmir (A Chronology of Events) -https://defence.pk/pdf/threads/history-of-kashmir-a-chronology-of-events.19185/

[6] Kashmir - Chronology of Major Events - http://www.peacekashmir.org/jammu-kashmir/jk-chronology-of-major-events.htm

[7] Ibid

[8] Ibid

[9] Kashmir - Chronology of Major Events - http://www.peacekashmir.org/jammu-kashmir/jk-chronology-of-major-events.htm

This was the main bone of contention that have contributed to the unrest and conflict in this part of the globe. In Indian occupied Kashmir there has been a freedom/insurgency movement to get rid of the illegal Indian occupation of Kashmir. With both India and Pakistan being nuclear powers, this conflict has the chance to spiral out of control and could lead to a catastrophic nuclear war. To resolve this, India needs to hold a plebiscite and let the Kashmir population choose their destiny.

Pakistan's dilemma

Pakistan's geography and location present its security planners with serious, almost irresolvable strategic and tactical problems. It borders the nuclear states of India and China, an ambitious Iran, and an unstable Afghanistan, which is perceived as a gateway to its commercial-strategic ambitions in Central Asia. Pakistan's key security problems are a reflection of its history and domestic circumstances. Located in a critical and historically contentious part of the world, Pakistan was composed of two wings, East Pakistan (renamed Bangladesh when it became independent in the 1971 war with India) and West Pakistan from its birth in 1947.[10]

The overriding concern of Pakistan is its internal and external security. Strategically, Pakistan lacks territorial depth. Its main cities and communication routes are relatively close to the border with India and are susceptible to attack. In addition, the headwater of Pakistan's rivers and main irrigation systems originate from India. Pakistan's borders with India were also new and mainly unfortified and, in many places, were drawn in ways that made them indefensible. Because the borders were also un-demarcated, there was abundant chance for conflict.[11]

According to Pakistan, its major threats continue to arise from the immediate neighbourhood. Of utmost concern is the Indian threat and the status of Kashmir (the K in Pakistan's name). Since independence in 1947 Indian and Pakistan have gone to war three times,[12] conducted hundreds of other skirmishes and artillery exchanges, and have assisted separatist movements in each other's countries, primarily over the territorial issue of Kashmir.[13] Moreover this root cause between them has not only remained unresolved, but it is as hot and volatile as ever before. Both countries have nuclear weapons and if their bad neighbourly relations flare up any more, there is a serious risk that nuclear war could break out. India and Pakistan each claim that their nuclear weapons are intended to deter the other, but neither has ruled out the first use of these weapons.[14]

Both nations possess advanced military aircraft that would be capable of delivering nuclear weapons.[15] Of greater concern, because of their speed and invulnerability to conventional air-defence systems, are both nations' ballistic missiles.[16] Reports in 1997 indicated that India has possibly deployed, or at least was storing, conventionally armed Prithvi missiles in Punjab, very near the Pakistani border. These missiles reduce warning time on both sides to nearly zero, making any nuclear crisis extremely unstable. India and Pakistan could hit targets in each other's countries in less than three minutes.[17]

---

[10] Hafeez Malik, Dilemmas of National Security and Co-operation, The Macmillan Press Ltd, 1993, Pg1
[11] Mustaq Ali Khan, Pakistan Army Green Book, Ferozsons (Pvt) Ltd, 1990, Pg292
[12] Venon Hewit, The New International Politics of South Asia, Manchester University Press, 1997, Pg20
[13] Janes Defence Weekly (JDW), On the Line of Fire, Janes Information Group Ltd, 1998, Pg25
[14] David Albright and Tom Zamora, Indian and Pakistan go Nuclear, Bulletin of Atomic Scientists, 1989, Pg20
[15] Albright and Zamora, op cit:26
[16] JDW, Asia's Missile Race Hots Up, 1994m, Pg20
[17] Tarun Basu, Selective Sattelite Tracking of Missiles Alledged, India Abroad, 1997, Pg12

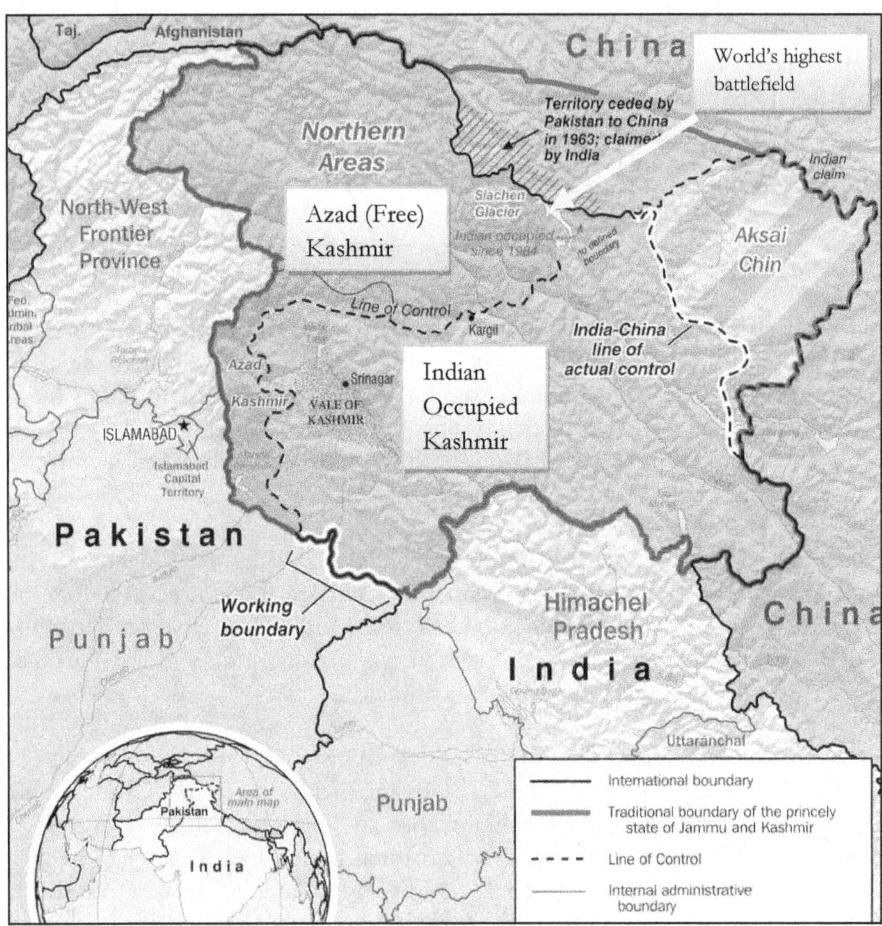

Disputed Area of Kashmir Map[18]

Although Pakistan perceived in India a threat to its security, initially it was not able to defend itself against that perceived threats because of limited personnel and material. In terms of all other key measurements such as size, population, resources, and general military strength, India holds an overwhelming advantage.[19] Pakistan therefore chose to develop a comprehensive military strategy that would offset at least some of its weaknesses. High hopes were placed on support from other Muslim nations, some of which could help financially and others of which would provide through alliances some of the geo-strategic territorial depth that Pakistan lacked.[20]

Pakistan's vision is to portray itself as a moderate Islamic state as a buffer against extremist Iran, chaos in Afghanistan and uncertainty in Central Asia. However, the rise of religious fundamentalist influences in recent years, particularly the growth of Hindu fundamentalism in India symbolised by the popularity of the militant Bharatiya Janata Party **(BJP)**, have greatly heightened tensions. Kashmir and Afghanistan are also a continuous problem, and internal social unrest has been blamed on outside factors, continuing the threat to Pakistan's security.[21]

Pakistan soldiers load an artillery piece to be fired at Indian positions from the Siachen Glacier

---

[18] http://legacy.lib.utexas.edu/maps/middle_east_and_asia/kashmir_disputed_2002.jpg
[19] Peter G. Tsourus, Changing Orders-The Evolution of the World's Armies, Arms and Armour Press, 1994, Pg 59
[20] Malik, op cit:133
[21] JDW, A Loss of Momentum, 1997, Pg 41

Pakistan military enhancing security measures in the country

Pakistani soldiers use multi-barrel rocket launchers to hit their targets during a military exercise

Chapter 2: The Pakistan – India Relationship

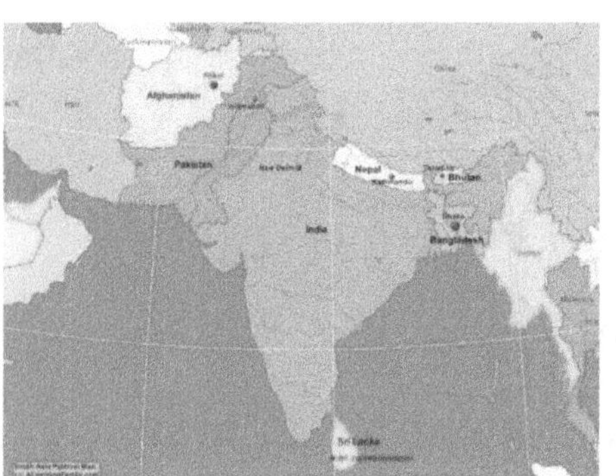

The Pakistan- India Relationship

Pakistan's principal security concern lies with its neighbour, India. Tensions have existed between India and Pakistan since Pakistan's creation in 1947. The partition of the Indian sub-continent also left Pakistan in two separate divisions- named East and West Pakistan, but separated by thousands of miles of Indian territory.[22] In 1947-48 the two countries fought a war over the disputed territory of Kashmir, which ended with Kashmir divided between them. A second war erupted in 1965, originating in the Ran of Kutch area and eventually spreading to Kashmir prompting India to launch a full scale invasion of West Pakistan in September 1965.[23]

Hostility between India and Pakistan deepened in 1970 over the problems of East Pakistan (Bangladesh), eventually leading to the 1971 Indo-Pakistan war and the subsequent dismemberment

---

[22] Lawrence Freedman, Atlas of Global Strategy, Macmillan Press Ltd, 1985, Pg 152
[23] Ibid

of Pakistan after its defeat. This event strengthened in many Pakistani minds the conviction that India was bent on the destruction of their country and its re-absorption into India, thinking which is still paramount in most government circles.[24]

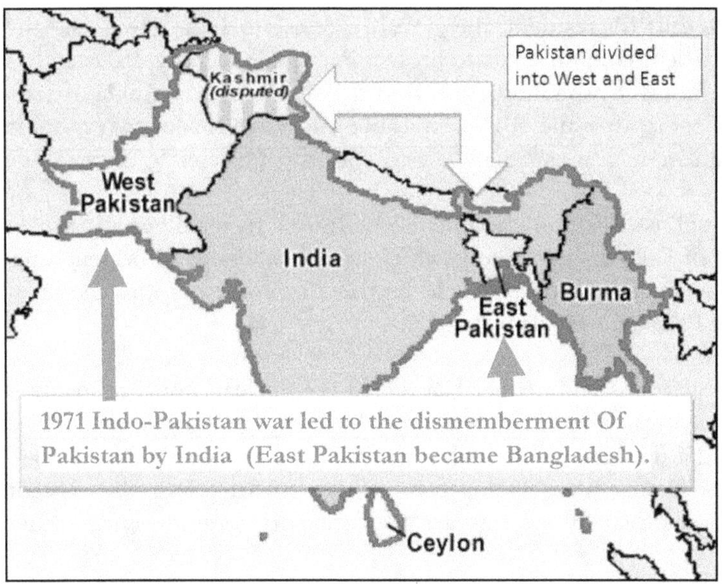

1971 Indo-Pakistan war led to the dismemberment Of Pakistan by India (East Pakistan became Bangladesh).

Pakistan's relations with India are marked by mutual distrust, divergence in foreign policy goals, and period tension. The current bitterness between Pakistan and India can be ascribed to a number of events. They include India's desire to play a dominant role in South Asia and its efforts to put down the nationalist struggle in Kashmir,[25] the conventional and nuclear arms race, the Siachin glacier (another issue which focuses on the demarcation of an area of common frontier left unclear in the Simla Agreement of 1972); the construction of Wuller Barrage on river Jhelum in Kashmir, which involves access to water resources; a disagreement over the Sir Creek boundary- a frontier demarcation dating from partition with implications on maritime territory; and charges of interference in each other's internal affairs.[26]

The strains caused by these problems are the major constraints on any effort to improve their bilateral relations.

Regional Hegemony

As the largest country in South Asia, India has continued to set the tone and define the parameters of inter-state relations within its region. Since 1971, this has involved it openly seeking short-term regional pre-eminence, as well as global power projection in the long-term. Encouraged by its size, the commitment of its people and by the huge military machine and its disposal, Delhi has consistently sought to conduct relations with its South Asian neighbours on its own terms. In the process, successive Indian governments have candidly deployed policy tools ranging from interventions to annexation and from subversions to economic blockades, to promote India's own policy goals (Sikkim 1970, troops into Sri Lanka in 1987 and in Maldives in 1988, and the economic blockade of Nepal 1989).[27]

This assertive role has caused considerable tension with Pakistan. In November 1986, India launched its largest military exercise ever, Operation Brass Tacks, close to the Pakistan border. The Pakistan Army responded with threatening counter-movements, raising serious concern that war might break out. An India-Pakistan hot line was set up after this. In May 1990, the uprising in Kashmir again brought the armies of Pakistan and India very close to conflict.[28] Tensions have continued due to the heavy handed and brutal tactics that India has done to the Kashmiri people in Indian occupied Kashmir. The Kashmiri separatist/freedom fighter, Burhan Wani's death on July 9, 2016 has sparked mass protests, with over 50,000 people congregated to mourn his death and joined his funeral procession.[29] With Indian development of Cold Start Doctrine (CSD) and a hawkish government – serious border firing has led to extreme tensions, that has a potential to breakout into an all-out war with nuclear Pakistan.

The Hindu fundamentalist Bharatiya Janata Party (BJP) - led coalition government in India has continued with the development of nuclear weapons to further her hegemonic goals in the area. This was reflected in the three nuclear

---

[24] Ibid

[25] JDW, Country Survey-Pakistan, 1992, Pg31

[26] Ibid

[27] Malik, op cit:153

[28] Ibid

[29] Who Was Burhan Wani And Why Is Kashmir Mourning Him? - https://www.huffingtonpost.in/burhan-wani/who-was-burhan-wani-and-why-is-kashmir-mourning-him_a_21429499/

devices exploded on May 11, 1998 and another two on May 13, 1998 at Pokhran, in spite of general opposition to testing.[30]

Pakistan viewed India's post-nuclear test statements as intimidatory and threatening to its security. The change in the regional balance was immediately obvious, and despite calls for restraint, the global response to India's tests and the promise of military aid from the US were seen as insufficient commitments to protect Pakistan's security. Pakistan has always seen itself as a bulwark to India's regional hegemonistic aspirations, and thus decided to conduct nuclear tests of its own, on 28th May 1998. The Indian tests had come after the BJP party came into government two months earlier, on the strength of a mandate which made an Indian nuclear capability as a top priority if elected.[31]

The BJP appeared to base its approach on two assumptions- Pakistan's acceptance of India's regional hegemony if it was unable to match the nuclear tests; and the fragility of Pakistan's economy, which would be unable to bear an arms race even if it did have a nuclear capability. Either way, at least Pakistan would be faced to come out into the open about its nuclear status, with either result impacting on Pakistan's regional status.[32]

Since both are now capable of manufacturing nuclear weapons and neither has signed the nuclear Non-Proliferation Treaty (NPT), their disputes taken on added significance. Indian and Pakistani forces have engaged in sporadic battles over the control of the Siachen Glacier in Kashmir and a full scale limited mini-war in Kargil, and the Indo-Pakistani border remains heavily militarised, with frequent cross-border firing raising fears of a potential fourth war. Recent events make the situation even more precarious. Missile delivery systems are beginning to come on-line, further heightening relations.[33]

Background to the India-Pakistan Conflict.

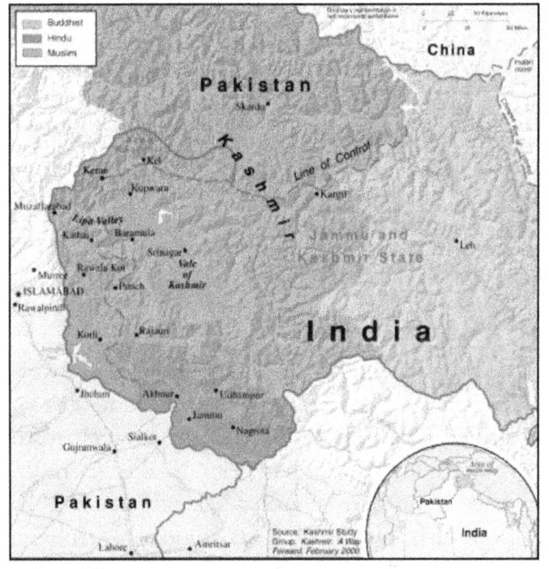

Kashmir Disputed Territory - Ethnic Mix Map[34]

Since their independence as new nations, India and Pakistan have followed a path of mutual animosity. Pakistan was created as a national homeland for the Muslim majority areas of the subcontinent, while India proposed to become a secular nation that included about 85% Hindus. Soon after the partition of the sub-continent into the two nations, millions of people fled their homes and journeyed to either Pakistan or India. In one of the largest exchanges of populations in history, violence soon broke out with Muslims on one side and Sikhs and Hindus on the other. The resulting bloodshed in the Punjab and West Bengal left more than a million dead.

In the midst of this refugee movement and open violence, the governments of India and Pakistan hastily tried to divide the assets of British India between the two new countries. Because the British had left behind (besides about half of the subcontinent which it directly governed) some 584 independent or 'princely states' with the provision that each state could either remain independent, join Pakistan or accede to India, a violent competition soon resulted as the two new nations sought to win the largest and most strategically located states, such as Hyderabad and Kashmir. Because Kashmir was more than 85% Muslim, Pakistan insisted that a vote be taken in the state.[35]

---

[30] JDW, India becomes Sixth Nuclear Weapons State, 1998, Pg4
[31] The Daily Telegraph, Nuclear Blasts Puts Pakistan in Arms Race, 1998, Pg1
[32] The Times, Pakistan Blasts into the Arms Race, Times Newspaper Ltd, 1998, Pg1
[33] JDW, Latest Tests put India in Nuclear Arms Spotlight, 1998, Pg3
[34] http://legacy.lib.utexas.edu/maps/middle_east_and_asia/jammu_kashmir_ethnic_2000.jpg
[35] Malik, op cit:6

The problem of Kashmir arose because the ruler of Kashmir, Maharaja Hari Singh, was unable to make up his mind to which dominion the state of Kashmir should accede to or whether to accede at all. The Maharajah's indecision furthered the interest of territorial gains by both nations, as Kashmir was a vital strategic asset, both religiously and territorially.[36]

The 85% majority of Muslims in Kashmir had no bearing on the outcome of events. Pakistan's claim to the kingdom seemed to be justified on the basis of the two nation theory. However, following implicit Pakistani support for the tribal invasion into the valley to help their fellow Muslims, the Maharaja signed up to join India and received immediate military help. This led to outrage in Pakistan and an immediate conflict between the two nations.[37]

The Hindu Maharaja accepted union with India and also Indian military assistance to quell a Pakistani effort to incorporate Kashmir. When India annexed the territory, Pakistan refused to acknowledge the unilateral move and invaded. The result was Indian control of roughly two-thirds of Kashmir, with Pakistani jurisdiction over the remaining third (Azad Kashmir), separated by a United Nations negotiated Line of Control. Despite two more wars and the signing of the 1972 Simla Agreement which mandated a bilateral settlement to resolve the issue, there has been no real progress on the Kashmir issue.[38]

The first war over Kashmir resulted in India taking the issue to the UN Security Council, which held passed a resolution that Kashmir's future be decided by a plebiscite under UN auspices.[39] India agreed on this UN-led resolution, but has since failed to implement the plebiscite, which called for a referendum of the Kashmir people to decide their future, on the grounds that Pakistan, by entering into a military alliance with the USA, had altered the region's security environment. It also claimed that UN resolutions were outdated, and that Kashmir was an integral part of India. Pakistan rejected this, and has never considered the status of Kashmir to have been settled.[40] **"We have no desire to impose our will on Kashmir…. Our assurance is that we shall withdraw our forces from Kashmir… and leave the decision regarding the future of this state (about its accession to India or Pakistan) to the people… through the democratic method of free and impartial plebiscite under the auspices of the United Nation. Those pledges have given not only to the people of Kashmir (and the government of Pakistan), but also to the world. We will not and cannot back out for it".[41]** Prime Minister of India, Jawaharlal Nehru

Bone of contention: India, Pakistan in legal skirmishes over Kashmir[42]

The 1965 war was also over Kashmir. For Pakistan, Kashmir is the sole bone of contention with India, claiming that the Indian occupation of Kashmir contravenes violates and defies the principles and basis of post-independence India and the two-nation theory which called for each state to decide its allegiance with either India or Pakistan according to its religious fabric. Pakistan argues that India has denied the rights of self-determination to the people of Kashmir, which is inherent in the UN

---

[36] Malik, op cit: 7

[37] Malik, op cit: 10

[38] Malik, op cit:165

[39] Malik, op cit:169

[40] Dawn Weekly, Kashmir Policy, Touch Media Co.Ltd, 1998, Pg14

[41] Dawn Weekly, Kashmir Policy, Touch Media Co.Ltd, 1998, Pg14

[42] http://dunyanews.tv/en/Pakistan/337369-Bone-of-contention-India-Pakistan-in-legal-skirm

Charter and UN Resolutions on Kashmir. In addition, India (according to Pakistan), having carried out intensive subversion in East Pakistan, exploited a great opportunity to forcibly dismember Pakistan. These events are an unforgettable part of Pakistan's history, and have a bearing on its people's psyche. Indian hostility, intentions and attitudes, and enhanced military preparations have a direct bearing on Pakistan's national security.[43]

At present, the Kashmir dispute is the most critical region of Indo-Pakistani security concern. Neither India nor Pakistan is satisfied with the status-quo and further violence is likely. The disputed territory entered a new phase of unrest in December 1989, with a programme of civil disobedience and wide popular support for various separatist groups in Indian-held Kashmir. Both states see the competition for influence in Kashmir as being of the utmost strategic importance.[44]

The massive uprising by the Kashmiris has resulted in India placing over 700,000 regular and paramilitary troops in the region in an attempt to curb the demands for implementation of the UN plebiscite. The uprising resulted in widespread allegations of torture, rape, killings and house burnings instigated by the Indian army. Amnesty International has collected much evidence on the atrocities committed, although for many years foreigners were restricted from entering Indian-held Kashmir. India insists that the Kashmir issue must be settled through bilateral discussions with Pakistan, while Pakistan encourages international involvement. For Pakistan the vacation of Kashmir by India is crucial imperative for its defence, and therefore its national security will remain threatened as long as Indian troops remain in Occupied Kashmir.[45]

PAF JF-17 Thunder combat aircraft

---

[43] Impact International, Kashmir after 48 years, News and Media Ltd, 1996, Pg7
[44] Ibid
[45] Ibid

Pakistan Army artillery in action

A brief history of the Indo-Pakistan Wars

India and Pakistan have gone to war a number of times, primarily due to the disputed territory of Kashmir. They have fought 3 major wars (1947,1965 and 1971) and 2 minor (limited) wars (Siachin glacier and Kargil). Pakistan and India had achieved independence from the British on August 15, 1947. The areas were split into predominantly Muslim or Hindu areas – but left many in the opposite side. This had resulted in a mass scale of killings, with each group vying to move into the newly established states. Mass migration took place as people moved to the countries corresponding to their religions. The majority of the Muslim-dominated princely states chose to join Pakistan, and Hindu-dominated princely states joined India, with some exceptions – this had contributed to the hostility between India and Pakistan to this date.[46]

---

[46] Indo-Pakistani War - https://www.worldatlas.com/articles/indo-pakistan-wars-1947-1965-1971-1999.html
India-Pakistan Wars, The Columbia Encyclopedia, 6th ed. - https://www.encyclopedia.com/history/asia-and-africa/south-asian-history/india-pakistan-wars
War History - https://www.pakistanarmy.gov.pk/AWPReview/TextContent.aspx?pId=47&rnd=443

Indo-Pakistan War of 1947-48

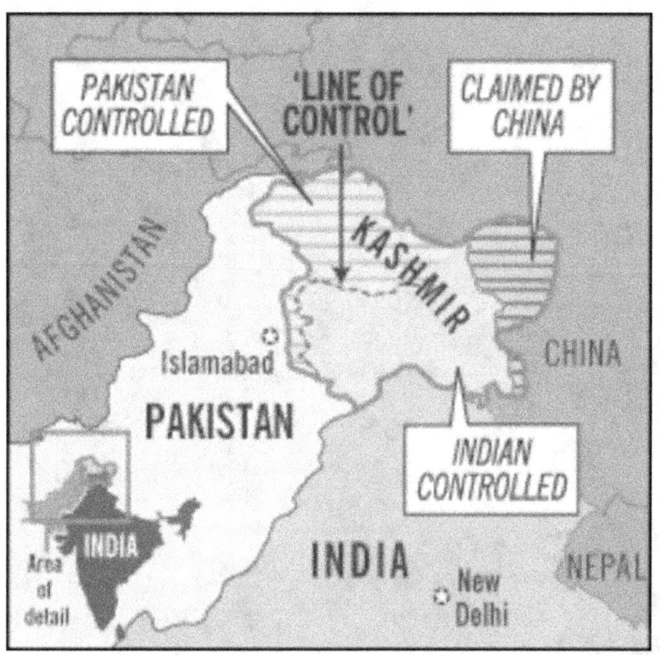

The First Indo-Pakistan war occurred shortly after independence when the Muslim majority of population wanted to unite with Pakistan, but its ruling Hindu Maharaja Hari Singh chose to side with Hindu India. In India's hyderabad state the ruler was a Muslim who had wanted to side with Pakistan but its majority hindu population did not want to and hence the the state was absorbed by India. In Pakistan's case the Kashmir should have been an integral part of the new state due to the wish and desire of its muslim majority population. Pakistan had always refused to recognise Jammu and Kashmir as an Indian state.

When the Hindu Maharaja of Kashmir was seen to be siding with India, his majority muslim population violently rebelled and demanded to join Pakistan. When the violence became too much for Hari Singh, he asked for Indian help and due to its support it agreed to accede Jammu and Kashmir to India. To support the Kasmiris desire to join with Pakistan, troops from Pakistan were sent to help the muslim majority state. A fully fledged conflict erupted between the two new countries, resulting in Pakistan taking control of Azad Kashmir and India taking Jammu, Ladakh and Kashmir valley.[47]

Indo-Pakistani War of 1965

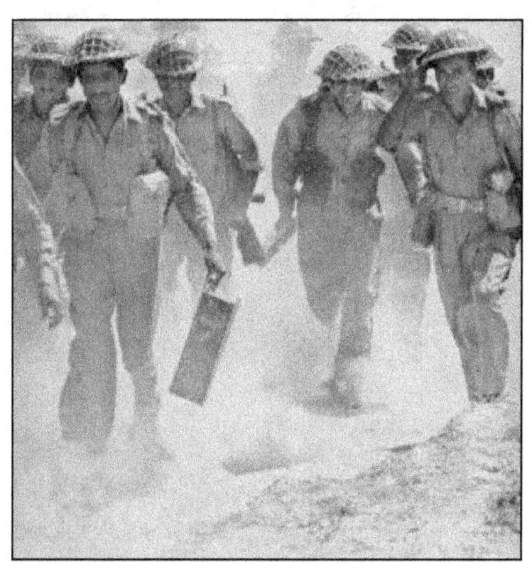

The Indo-Pakistan war of 1965 started when Indian forces tried to take the disputed Rann of Kutch region in April. With short intense conflict in this area the Indian troops were ejected from this region. A cease-fire was agreed by both sides to reduce the tensions. By August 1965 , fighting between India and Pakistan spread to Kashmir and to the Punjab regions, and on 5/6 September, without a formal declaration of war, Indian Army crossed the international border and attacked Lahore and Kasur fronts. Pakistan Army and Pakistan Air Force halted the attack in its tracks, inflicting heavy casualties on the aggressor. On 7 September a single Pakistan Air Force Pilot, Squadron Leader M.M. Alam, Sitara-i-Juraat, in his F-86 Sabre shot down five Indian Air Force attacking Hunter aircraft in a single sortie, an unbeaten world record. Both Pakistani and Indian troops crossed the partition line between the two countries and launched air assaults on each other's cities. Although this war only lasted for 17 days, it resulted in thousands of deaths. The war was the largest grouping of troops since independence and the largest tank battle since World War II. As soon as the presence of Indian 1 Armoured Division was confirmed,

---

[47] Indo-Pakistani War - https://www.worldatlas.com/articles/indo-pakistan-wars-1947-1965-1971-1999.html
India-Pakistan Wars, The Columbia Encyclopedia, 6th ed. - https://www.encyclopedia.com/history/asia-and-africa/south-asian-history/india-pakistan-wars
War History - https://www.pakistanarmy.gov.pk/AWPReview/TextContent.aspx?pId=47&rnd=443

Pakistan Army rushed forward to stop the onslaught on a 30-mile front. The biggest tank battle since World War II was fought on the Chwinda front by 6 Armoured Division with under command 24 Infantry Brigade Groups and valiantly supported by 4 Corps Artillery (Brigadier A.A.K. Choudhry, Hilal-i-Juraat). The main effort of the Indian Army was blunted, inflicting heavy and troop casualties. Pakistan Air Force support helped turn the tide of the battle. Pakistan and India agreed to a UN-sponsored cease-fire and withdrew to the pre-August lines.[48]

Front Page of Australia's Leading Newspaper on Sept 11, 1965[49]

Indo-Pakistan War of 1971

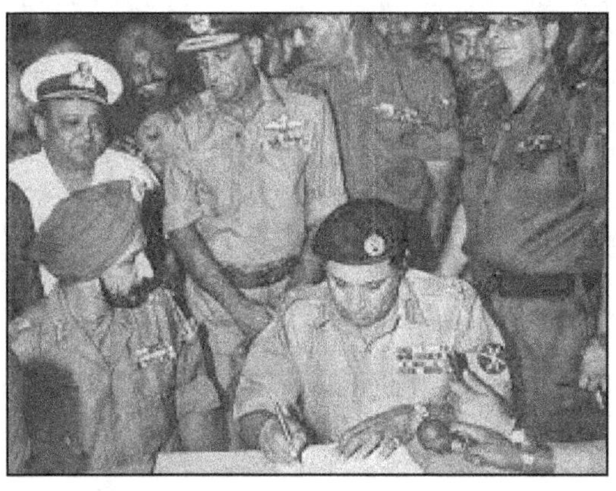

Lieutenant General A. A. K. Niazi (right) signing the Instrument of Surrender while surrendering to Lieutenant General Jagjit Singh Arora of the Indian Army in 1971.

The 1971 Indo-Pakistan was the first war that did not involve fighting over the Kashmir region. Pakistan consisted of 2 parts – West Pakistan and East Pakistan. Political instability and poor governorship in West Pakistan led to resentment of the East Pakistani population. In March of 1971, an East Pakistan political party won the election, and West Pakistan chose not to recognize the results. This decision led to political unrest in East Pakistan, and West Pakistan responded with military force. India had seen this as an opportunity to cause mayhem and mischief for Pakistan. India conducted psychological

[48] Indo-Pakistani War - https://www.worldatlas.com/articles/indo-pakistan-wars-1947-1965-1971-1999.html
India-Pakistan Wars, The Columbia Encyclopedia, 6th ed. - https://www.encyclopedia.com/history/asia-and-africa/south-asian-history/india-pakistan-wars
War History - https://www.pakistanarmy.gov.pk/AWPReview/TextContent.aspx?pId=47&rnd=443
[49] Who Won the 1965 War? - http://www.riazhaq.com/2016/09/who-won-1965-war-india-or-pakistan.html

operations and militarily supported the rebel 'Mukti Bahini' against Pakistani troops in East Pakistan. Pakistan pursued in hot pursuit of the rebel forces who were aided by India.

India's covert armed intervention was causing serious issues on the security of East Pakistan. Accordingly, by October India had amassed a force four times Pakistan's strength in over 12 divisions (400,000) supported by five regiments of tanks, and about 50,000 activists trained and equipped by Indian Army. Indian Navy's one aircraft carrier, eight destroyers/frigates, two submarines and three landing craft, against our four gunboats, eight Chinese coasters and two landing craft supported them. Eleven Indian Air Force squadrons – 4 Hunter, 1 SU-7, 3 Gnat and 3 MiG 21 – from five airfields around East Pakistan faced our one valiant Number 14 squadron of F-86F Sabres based on a single airfield around Dhaka. The Pakistan armed forces had put a strong resistance and caused heavy casualties on the Indian Forces, but India's numerical advantages (with the support of the rebel Mukhti Bahini groups/insurgency) gradually resulted in dismembering Pakistan – with East Pakistan declaring independence as Bangladesh.

India's Field Marshal Sam Manekshaw's interview with Karan Thapur on BBC's Face-to-Face programme about the 1971 Indo-Pakistan war, stated the following:

"About the 5th day of the (1971) conflict in (East Pakistan)...everything had gone wrong (for India); the (Indian) Navy had lost the Khukri; Our (India) Air Force has lost a lot of aircraft on the ground; my (Indian Army's) advances in Bangladesh were halted......The Pakistan Army in East Pakistan fought very gallantly but they had no chance; they were a thousand miles away from their base; I had 8 or 9 months of preparation; I had almost 50:1 advantage; they had no chance but they fought very gallantly."[50]

In addition, the Legendary USAF pilot General Chuck Yeager observed the performance of the Pakistan Air Force in the 1971 war. In his autobiography 'The Right Stuff', he said the following:

"This air force (the PAF), is second to none...The (1971) air war lasted two weeks and the Pakistanis scored a three-to-one kill ratio, knocking out 102 Russian-made Indian jets and losing thirty-four airplanes of their own. I'm certain about the figures because I went out several times a day in a chopper and counted the wrecks below...They were really good, aggressive dogfighters and proficient in gunnery and air combat tactics. I was damned impressed. Those guys just lived and breathed flying."[51]

India was supporting the insurgency and was fomenting the breakaway of Pakistan. The Indian Prime Minister, Indira Ghandi decided to intervene in the civil war, supporting an independent Bengali state. India began supporting rebel troops in Bangladesh, in response, Pakistan attacked an Indian military base in December of 1971. This attack was the official start of the war. Under great-power pressure, a UN cease-fire was arranged in mid-December, after Pakistan's defeat. Pakistan lost its eastern half, an army of 93,000 soldiers (though some analysts believe the real figure was between 45,000 – 50,000),[52] and was thrown into political turmoil. Zulfikar Ali Bhutto emerged as leader of Pakistan, and Mujibur Rahman as prime minister of Bangladesh. This was a disaster for Pakistan and a number of findings were undertaken to see where things had gone wrong. For Pakistan, it was now convinced that India would take any opportunity to destroy and dismantle Pakistan – it had to ensure that it had the means to deter this threat from India and its regional hegemonistic tendencies.[53]

Indo-Pakistan Mini-War of 1984 – Siachin Glacier (Highest battlefield in the world - Kashmir)

---

[50] Indo-Pakistan War - http://www.riazhaq.com/2016/09/performance-of-pakistan-armed-forces-in.html

[51] Video clip of Sam Manekshaw speaking with Karan Thapar on 1971 war - https://www.youtube.com/watch?v=W8I1lk1A-aE&t=36s Indo-Pakistan War - http://www.riazhaq.com/2016/09/performance-of-pakistan-armed-forces-in.html

[52] 93,000 Pakistani soldiers did not surrender in 1971 because....? - https://www.globalvillagespace.com/93000-pakistani-soldiers-did-not-surrender-in-1971-because/

[53] Video clip of Sam Manekshaw speaking with Karan Thapar on 1971 war - https://www.youtube.com/watch?v=W8I1lk1A-aE&t=36s **Indo-Pakistan War** - http://www.riazhaq.com/2016/09/performance-of-pakistan-armed-forces-in.html

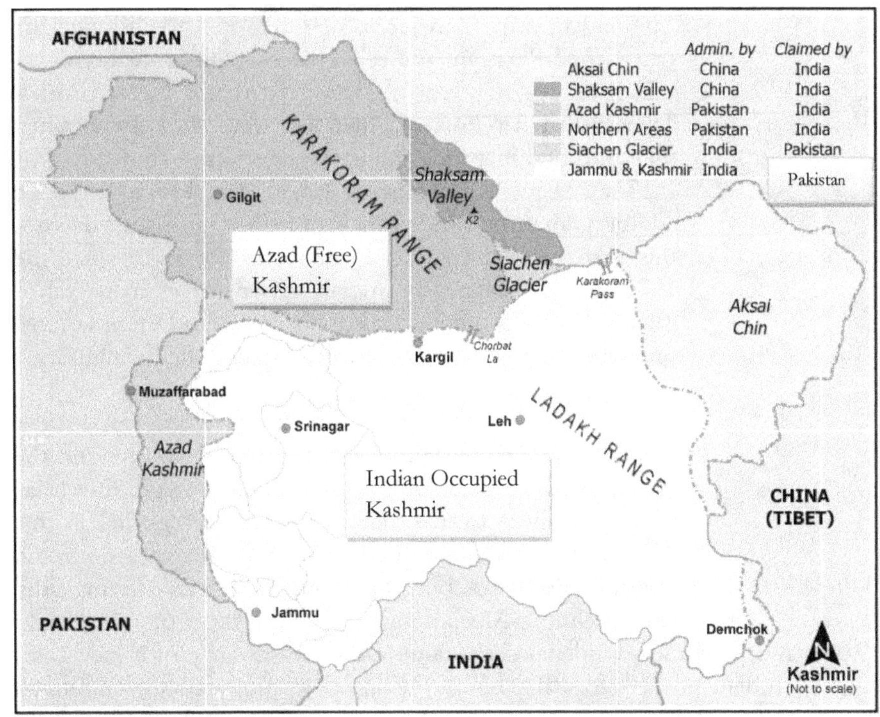

The Siachin Glacier in disputed Kashmir became the highest battlefield in the world, when Indian troops snatched control of the Siachin Glacier, only narrowly beating Pakistan. In April 1984, India conducted 'Operation Meghdoot' and took control of Siachin glacier. The world's highest battle (high-altitude trench warfare) is moving into its fourth decade, with opposing armies in the same positions as 30 years ago. Battles have occurred here in-excess of 22,000 ft.[54]

Over 2,700 Indian and Pakistani troop deaths have been mainly due to the extreme weather in the area rather than actual combat – avalanches, exposure and altitude sickness have been the primary cause of death (the high areas have oxygen-depleted air)[55]

The natural hazards of mountain warfare has taken its gradual toll on both Indian and Pakistani forces in the area. The Siachen Glacier was named the highest battleground in the world with both the countries holding their respective positions at nearly 7 km above sea level.[56] The conflict is causing a widespread loss of life and escalating cost of war (due to the supply of equipment in these remote areas). The huge high-altitude military struggle between India and Pakistan has continued unabated to the present day.[57]

Indo-Pakistan Mini-War of 1999 – Kargil Conflict (Kashmir)

The Kargil war took place between May and July 1999 and was a limited mini-war between India and Pakistan. This mini-war had the potential to spread out across the international border between India and Pakistan and could have resulted in a full scale war. Since both countries had tested their nuclear devices earlier, there was a very high risk that an all-out nuclear war could take place – due to the disparities of the armed forces in the region. It started when Kashmiri rebels (Freedom fighters) occupied vacated Indian posts across the line of control (Kargil district). Pakistan had sent its troops to support the rebels and India retaliated with a major military response.

---

[54] Siachin Glacier - http://www.siachenglacier.com/pakistanperspective.html

[55] Siachen dispute: India and Pakistan's glacial fight - http://www.bbc.co.uk/news/world-asia-india-26967340

[56] Siachin Glacier - http://www.siachenglacier.com/mountain-warfare.html

[57] Pakistan Army - https://www.pakistanarmy.gov.pk/

The Indian army and air force attempted to dislodge the entrenched Pakistani and rebel forces. Significant firepower was used but it was a hard slog to regain the territories. Two Indian Air Force fighter jets were shot down when they intruded in to the Pakistani air space – shot down by Pakistani army air defences (Anza Manpad system).[58] In addition, an armed Indian helicopter was also shot down – this was the first significant air losses for India since the 1971 Indo-Pakistan war. Indian armed forces managed to retake most of the occupied positions and International pressure was put on both countries to end the hostilities.

One of the main Pakistani aim in this mini-war border conflict was to Internationalise the conflict and remind the World of the outstanding UN resolutions that India has failed to adhere to in order to resolve the conflict in this region. India has attempted to portray this as a domestic internal issue – but in reality it fears giving the overwhelming Muslim majority population of its right to determine its own choice (either to Join Pakistan or become an independent state). Other reason given for Pakistan - it supported the infiltrators that had occupied Indian posts across the Line of Control to put pressure on Indian forces to withdraw from the Siachin glacier area (withdrawal from Siachin in exchange for Kargil).[59] The Kargil conflict resulted in a loss of life for both sides, but India losing a significant numbers - rough estimates show that the Indian army has lost more officers and men in these few weeks of fighting in Kargil than it lost in the last full-fledged war with Pakistan in 1971.[60] International pressure resulted in the end of the conflict – as the outside world feared that things were getting out of hand and it could lead to a catastrophic nuclear exchange between both countries.

Kargil Conflict 1999

Indian Mig-27 Flogger Strike aircraft

IAF Mig-21 Fishbed combat aircraft

---

[58] Indian jets shot down by Pakistan - https://www.independent.co.uk/news/indian-jets-shot-down-by-pakistan-1096382.html

[59] Ganguly, Sumit; Kapur, S. Paul (2012). India, Pakistan, and the Bomb: Debating Nuclear Stability in South Asia, Columbia University Press. p. 50.

[60] When Pakistan and India went to war over Kashmir in 1999 - https://herald.dawn.com/news/1153481

Indian helicopter gunship - Mi-17 was shot down by Pakistani air defence. India's Mi-17 gunship was hit by the surface-to-air missile at 16,000 feet in Kashmir's remote Kargil region.[61]

Pak Army soldiers with the tail of Indian MiG-21 fighter jet

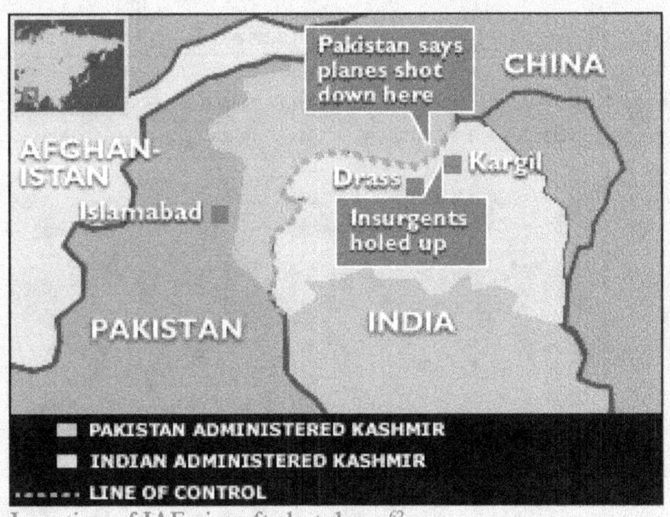

Location of IAF aircraft shot down[62]

Pak Army soldiers with the tail of Indian MiG-21 fighter jet in Hunzi Ghund in Pakistan territory - both IAF jets were shot inside Pakistan territory which were involved in hostile attack.

---

[61] Tensions heighten after Indian helicopter is shot down by Stinger missile - https://www.irishtimes.com/news/tensions-heighten-after-indian-helicopter-is-shot-down-by-stinger-missile-1.190163

[62] India loses two jets - http://news.bbc.co.uk/1/hi/world/south_asia/354120.stm#map

Anza man-portable air defence missile

Indo-Pakistan Border skirmishes and artillery duels

Indo-Pakistan tensions have existed since both countries achieved independence from British India. They have gone to war on a number of occasions and have had numerous border skirmishes and artillery duels. This has caused tensions to further flare up and loss of lives for the border troops as well as the civilian population on both side of the border. Many thousands have been injured over the years and this has caused more resentment from both sides.

Tensions have increased in Indian occupied Kashmiri where over 700,000 military/security personnel are suppressing the indigenous people of this part. Constant battles with local militants (who have local support of the people) and Indian security forces have intensified. There are numerous cases of genocide committed by Indian security forces (mass graves have been unearthed). The Indian's are using Israeli tactics in suppressing the local population. Israel continues to provide much expertise to its ally India in this area as it has tested these barbaric tactics to the Palestinian people over the many decades. In addition, fake news and false narratives are propagated by the Indian forces and media, and this has led to support from non-Muslim countries to the Indian cause. However, truth will always come out eventually and this is what is causing the Indian government, especially the fundamentalist BJP Hindu party of Prime Minister Modi a lot of issues. The attacks against Indian forces have been increasingly carried out by local militants, rebels willing to sacrifice their lives for freedom from Indian occupation and subjugation. The fear is that this region could lead to a catastrophic nuclear war between India and Pakistan if these issues are not amicably resolved.

Indian border troops

Pakistani border troops

Indian artillery men lift the turrets of the 155mm Bofors guns

Pakistani artillery men

Surgical strikes, nothing more than border skirmishes[63]

The analyst Riaz Haq (South Asia Investor Review) has stated the following, **"The essence of Kashmir issue today is not Uri or Pathankot or similar other alleged "militant attacks"; it is India's brutal military occupation force of 700,000 heavily-armed Indian soldiers being resisted by over 10 million Kashmiris. Anyone who tells you otherwise is a liar".**

---

[63] What Indian and Pakistani Newspapers Said About 'Surgical Strikes' Along Line of Control - https://blogs.wsj.com/indiarealtime/2016/09/30/what-indian-and-pakistani-newspapers-said-about-surgical-strikes-along-line-of-control/

According to Riaz Haq, **"Not only is the Indian government denying the right of self-determination granted to Kashmiris by multiple UN Security Council Resolutions, New Delhi is also reneging on the commitments made by India's founder and first prime minister Jawaharlal Nehru to Kashmiris and the international community"**.[64]

"...our assurance that we shall withdraw our troops from Kashmir as soon as peace and order is restored and leave the decision regarding the future of the State to the people of the State is not merely a promise to your Government but also to the people of Kashmir and to the world."

(Jawahar Lal Nehru, Telegram No. 25, October 31, 1947, to Liaqat Ali Khan, PM of Pakistan)

Indian Prime Minister Jawaharlal Nehru's Pledge[65]

Riaz further states, **"India is deploying 700,000 troops with extraordinary powers to detain, torture, blind, injure and kill any Kashmiri citizen with impunity under Armed Forces (Jammu and Kashmir) Special Powers Act 1990"**.

There is widespread evidence and documentation of state sponsored violence against the Kashmiris in India. Dr. Angana Chatterji, a professor of cultural and social anthropology at California Centre for Integral Studies, stated that the **"violence and militarization in Kashmir, between 1989-2009, have resulted in over 70,000 deaths, including through extrajudicial or fake encounter executions, custodial brutality, and other means"**. she further added. **"In the enduring conflict, 667,000 military and paramilitary personnel continue to act with impunity to regulate movement, law, and order across Kashmir,"** (The International Peoples' Tribunal on Human Rights and Justice).[66]

The many years of oppression in Indian occupied Kashmir has further contributed to the ill-feelings and desire of the Kashmiris to free themselves of Indian occupation of their land. New generation youngsters such as Burhan Wani and many others - who have only witnessed Indian occupation and repression against their people, have become more determined to resist the illegal military occupation of their land by India.[67]

Human rights activist Ajit Sahi has exposed on numerous occasions the atrocities in Kashmir committed by the Indian Prime Minister Modi's BJP fundamentalist government. Ajit Sahi says, "6 people a day being killed in extrajudicial killings". (Tom Lantos Human Rights Commission).[68] A lot of the suppression that the Indian army and security personnel have undertaken have been borrowed from the Israeli security forces in their brutality against the Palestinian people. Close military connection between Israel and India has increased significantly, with the support of sophisticated Israeli arms to quell any form of resistance in Indian occupied Kashmir. Many of the brutal tactics employed by the Indian army and security forces has been barbaric and have taken leaf from the Israeli expertise in subduing the Palestinian population. There are widespread evidence, of torture, mass rape comtitted by the Indian armed forces to humiliate and subjugate Kashmiri women. The use of rubber bullets/pellets and other extreme tools have caused widespread injuries and resentment amongst the Kashmiri population. India has used mass propaganda to project this as nothing more than 'terrorists' when evidence shows otherwise.

It is clear that these kind of suppression tactics will result in more Kashmiris taking up arms against the illegal Indian occupation of Indian held Kashmir.

---

[64] 700,000 Indian Soldiers Versus 10 Million Kashmiris - http://www.riazhaq.com/2016/09/700000-indian-soldiers-versus-10.html

[65] 700,000 Indian Soldiers Versus 10 Million Kashmiris - http://www.riazhaq.com/2016/09/700000-indian-soldiers-versus-10.html

[66] Ibid

[67] Ibid

[68] Human rights activist Ajit Sahi - https://www.youtube.com/watch?v=CBjfOERnLz0

India has started to use the same brutal tactics as the Israeli armed forces have done to the Palestinian people[69] There is a close military alliance between these two countries.

The systematic torture and human rights violations against the Kashmiri people in Indian occupied Kashmir has increased tensions between India and Pakistan. The Fear is that the brutal oppression in occupied Kashmir could become the catalyst for a major conflict with neighbouring Pakistan.

Brutal and heavy handed tactics by the Indian army/security forces (numbering over 700,000 troops) have further alienated the Kashmiri population – there are evidence of genocide (mass graves), torture, rape by Indian security forces, use of pellet guns blinding many people etc, - The Indian military forces are behaving like an occupying force and oppressing the basic human rights of the people in this area.[70]

---

[69] India must stop crimes against humanity in IOK: Sardar Masood Khan, Kashmir Watch - http://kashmirwatch.com/india-must-stop-human-right-violations-and-crimes-against-humanity-in-iok-sardar-masood-khan/
[70] Kashmir Conflict in Contemporary India - https://cafedissensusblog.com/2017/03/27/kashmir-conflict-in-contemporary-india/

Kashmir Death caused by the Indian Army

Many cases of extra judicial killings, missing people, uncovering of mass graves, thousands of Kashmiri women being raped as a means of humiliation and subjugation, widespread use of torture under the pretext of fake militant encounters – all undertaken by Indian military and security forces. Despite repeated claims of being the largest democracy in the world – none of this has been given to the Kashmiri people in Indian held Kashmir. There are widespread evidence of Indian atrocities available to the global media – but India's propaganda machine has successfully washed away these concerns.

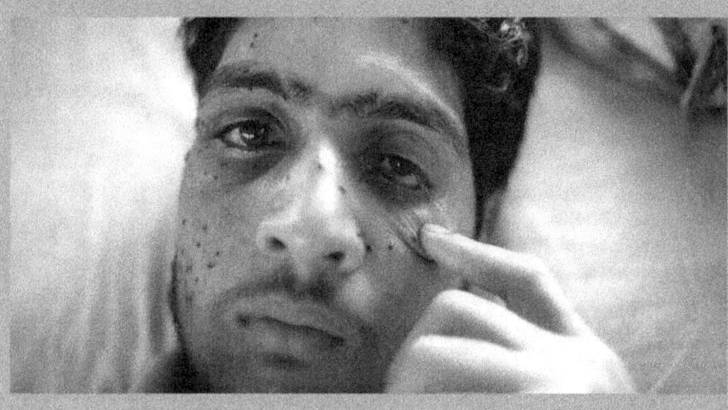

Pellet guns are deliberately used to blind protestors against the illegal occupation of Indian held Kashmir. There are cases of many individuals being blinded by these nasty weapons.

India has attempted to project these uprisings as terrorist movements when in fact it is no more than freedom movements to rid of Indian oppression in Indian occupied Kashmir. India blames Pakistan for causing the issues, but in reality it fears that if the people of Kashmir are given their rights to decide (as per UN resolution) then the Kashmiris will either join with Pakistan or become totally independent. Kashmir should have naturally joined with Pakistan at independence – but India's invasion of Kashmir under the pretext of Hari Singh (Hindu Maharaja of Kashmir) request for help (which was requested when the people of Kashmir rebelled against the decisions of Hari Singh to side with India). The Muslim majority population was illegally seized by Indian forces and should have naturally joined with Pakistan at its inception..

Evidence of mass rapes by Indian security forces in occupied Indian Kashmir has been documented by numerous human rights and government organisations.

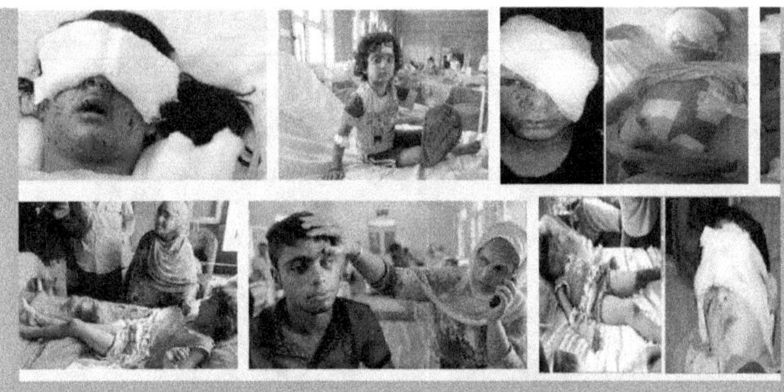

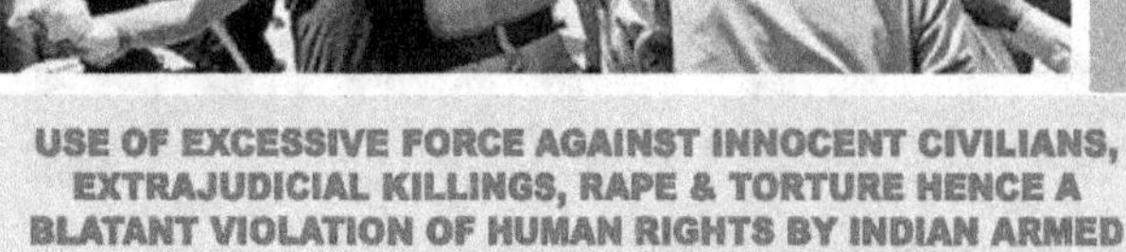

Evidence of torture and use of inhumane weapons to break the resistance movement in Indian held Kashmir. Due to India's rapid economic growth rates, foreign powers such as the USA and its allies have now started to turn a blind eye to these Indian atrocities and genocide being committed in this part of the world.

https://www.pinterest.co.uk/pin/393853929895656016/

USE OF EXCESSIVE FORCE AGAINST INNOCENT CIVILIANS, EXTRAJUDICIAL KILLINGS, RAPE & TORTURE HENCE A BLATANT VIOLATION OF HUMAN RIGHTS BY INDIAN ARMED FORCES IN INDIAN OCCUPIED KASHMIR

Excessive use of torture and killings have further alienated the Kasmiri people in Indian occupied Kashmir. India has the world's largest number of troops in one area – over 700,000 soldiers are used to subdue the people in this area.

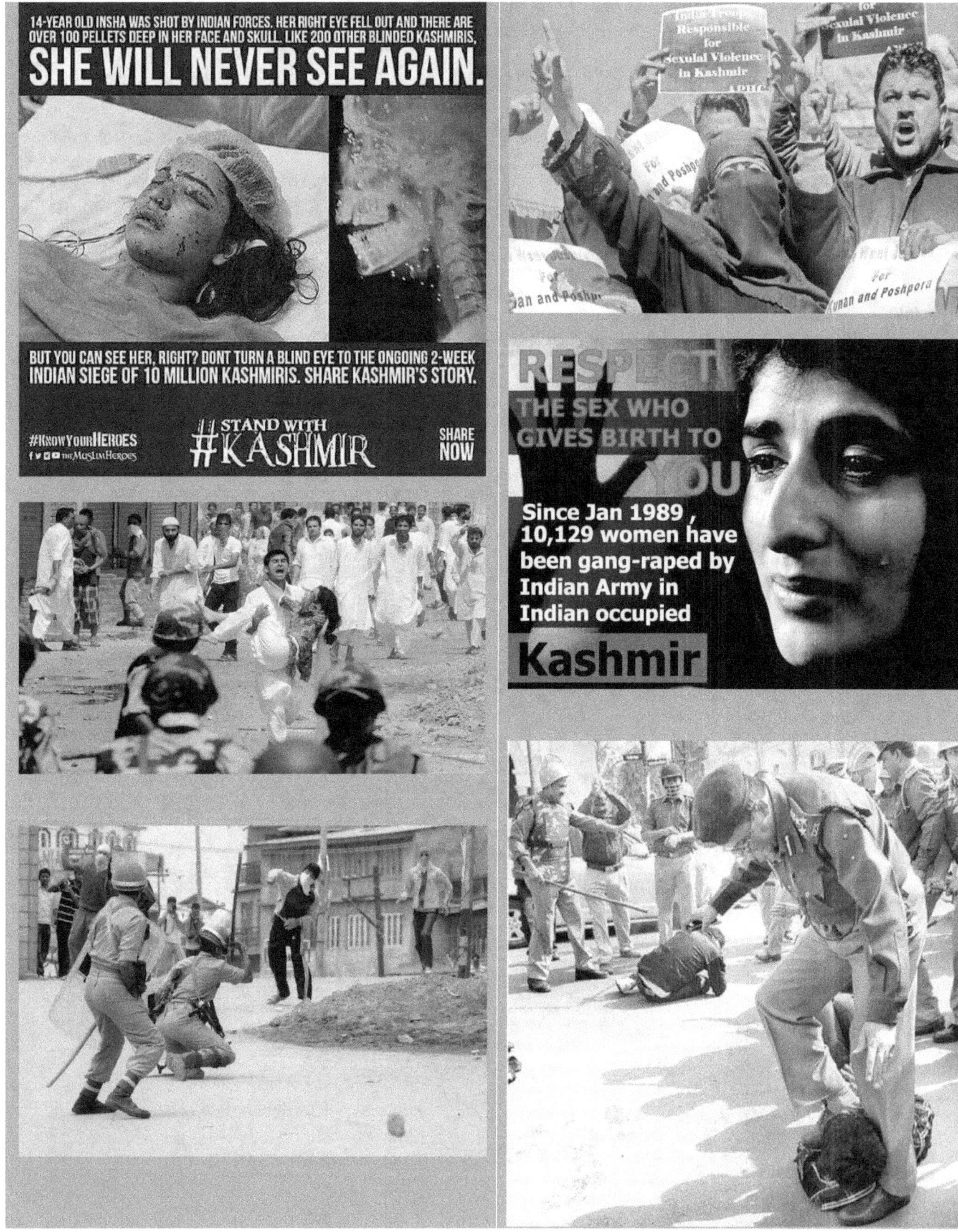
14-YEAR OLD INSHA WAS SHOT BY INDIAN FORCES. HER RIGHT EYE FELL OUT AND THERE ARE OVER 100 PELLETS DEEP IN HER FACE AND SKULL. LIKE 200 OTHER BLINDED KASHMIRIS,
SHE WILL NEVER SEE AGAIN.
BUT YOU CAN SEE HER, RIGHT? DONT TURN A BLIND EYE TO THE ONGOING 2-WEEK INDIAN SIEGE OF 10 MILLION KASHMIRIS. SHARE KASHMIR'S STORY.
#KnowYourHeroes
TheMuslimHeroes
#STAND WITH #KASHMIR
SHARE NOW
Indian Troops Responsible for Sexual Violence in Kashmir
for Sexual Violence in Kashmir
RESPECT THE SEX WHO GIVES BIRTH TO YOU
Since Jan 1989 , 10,129 women have been gang-raped by Indian Army in Indian occupied
Kashmir

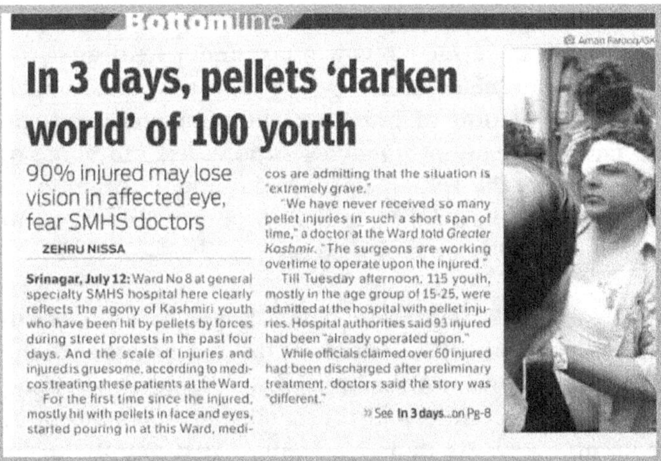

In 3 days, pellets 'darken world' of 100 youth

90% injured may lose vision in affected eye, fear SMHS doctors

ZEHRU NISSA

Srinagar, July 12: Ward No 8 at general specialty SMHS hospital here clearly reflects the agony of Kashmiri youth who have been hit by pellets by forces during street protests in the past four days. And the scale of injuries and injured is gruesome, according to medicos treating these patients at the Ward.

For the first time since the injured, mostly hit with pellets in face and eyes, started pouring in at this Ward, medicos are admitting that the situation is "extremely grave."

"We have never received so many pellet injuries in such a short span of time," a doctor at the Ward told *Greater Kashmir*. "The surgeons are working overtime to operate upon the injured."

Till Tuesday afternoon, 115 youth, mostly in the age group of 15-25, were admitted at the hospital with pellet injuries. Hospital authorities said 93 injured had been "already operated upon."

While officials claimed over 60 injured had been discharged after preliminary treatment, doctors said the story was "different."

» See **In 3 days**...on Pg-8

According Inamul Haq, (Phd student of Central University of Gujarat, India), **"The basic reason for the breakout of the violence was the rigged elections of 1987, followed by an armed revolt after, and had drawn the Kashmir Valley into the conflict zone. The state was put under undeclared emergency from the 1990s, which disrupted the values of rule of law and made possible the violation of human rights and restricted the fundamental freedom of the people of the Valley. The law enforcement agencies suppressed the voice of self-determination by using force and creating alienation towards the Indian state. The popular uprisings in 2008, 2010, and 2016 prove this alienation. The prominent laws like AFSPA and PSA gave a free hand to security forces in propagating cruel and inhuman treatments on the people of Kashmir"**.[71]

And further states. **"From July 09, 2016, the uprising after the death of Burhan Wani should be a matter of utmost concern not only for India, but the whole world. The approach adopted by the Indian state is the evidence that for India, there is only value of Kashmiri resources and not Kashmiris………… The demand of plebiscite, the slogans of Azaadi (freedom), the rage of stone-pelting and the raising of Pakistani flags showed the isolation people felt from India. There are so many events that clearly show that people in the Valley do not want to remain a part of India. Why are the educated youth in Kashmir, unlike the earlier militancy movements, picking up arms?"**.[72]

The disputed Kashmir has been the main bone of contention between India and Pakistan – majority of the issues between the 2 countries always are related to Kashmir region. Both sides need to amicably resolve this dispute and end the sufferings in this part of the world . India needs to adhere to its promise of giving the Kashmiris the right to self-determination that it had promised once it had invaded occupied kashmir at the behest of the Hindu Maharaja Hari Singh. The Hindu fundamentalist government of Prime Minister Modi need to stop fanning the flames of violence against non-hindus in India. Since the BJP government has been in power it has caused considerable tension in India amongst its different communities and in the region with its neighbours. Its desire of a 'hindutva' hindu nation and its pressure to try to 'hinduise its Christian, Muslim and other minorities' could cause an implosion within India and be a catalyst for a catastrophic war with its nuclear neighbour Pakistan. The fascist RSS group adheres to Nazi germany thinking, of which Prime minister Modi and his party are heavily influenced by (a lot of them have been members of the fascist group).

---

[71] Kashmir Conflict in Contemporary India - https://cafedissensusblog.com/2017/03/27/kashmir-conflict-in-contemporary-india/
[72] Ibid

Ex-soldier & UN Peacekeeper, Raghu Raman, states the following, **"For all the chauvinistic war mongering touted in every medium, India cannot 'win' a war against Pakistan and the sooner we appreciate this politico-military reality, the more coherent and serious we will sound to our adversaries and the world community. The demands for a 'once and for all' resolution of Kashmir/Pakistan emanating from several quarters, which surprisingly includes some veterans – equating India's non-retaliation with impotence – perhaps don't factor the larger picture and the stark truth of modern military warfare"**. He further contends, **"Matter of fact, short of total genocide, no country regardless of its war-withal can hope to achieve a decisive victory with a 'short war' in today's world. As the US is discovering eight years, trillion dollars and over 25,000 casualties later - in Afghanistan. That era of 'decisive' short wars – especially in context of an Indo-Pak war is largely over because of**

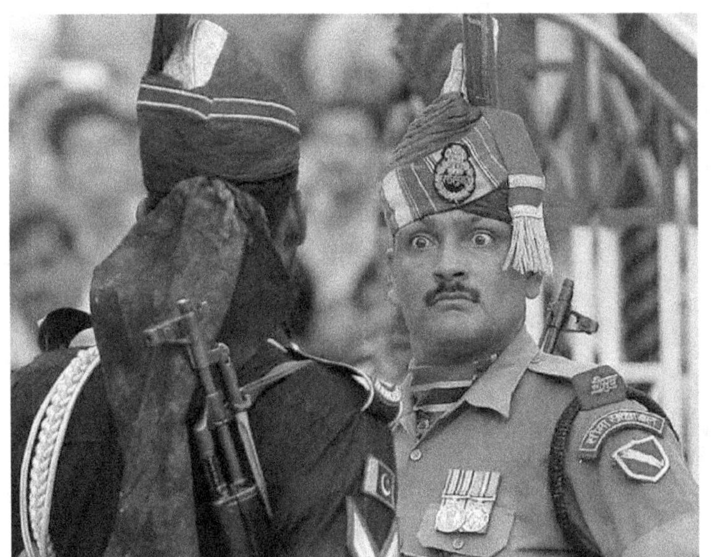

several reasons".[73]

India and Pakistan have to resolve the Kashmir issue amicably in order to avoid a never ending cycle of conflict. This conflict is having an adverse effect on the economies and the welfare of the people of South Asia.

Indian Soldiers on a border patrol

---

[73] Raghu Raman, Why war with Pakistan—is not an option - https://medium.com/@captraman/why-war-with-pakistan-is-not-an-option-3ccfa25a1529

Chapter 3: Kashmir Scenario – Potential for a nuclear war

The Indo-Pakistan dispute over Kashmir has great potential for miscalculations to occur, this could have a disastrous impact for the region. The risks of inadvertent nuclear war becomes more likely – with serious global ramifications. The following is a likely scenario in Kashmir that could easily escalate to a nuclear exchange for India and Pakistan.

Kashmir Scenario – Potential for a nuclear war

Freedom demands from Indian occupation – Civil disturbances

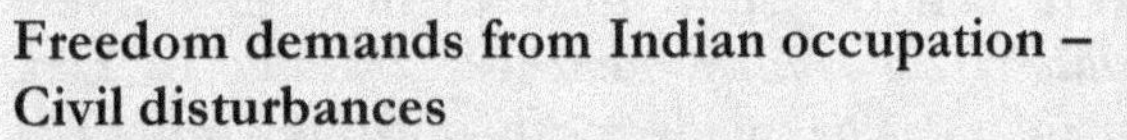
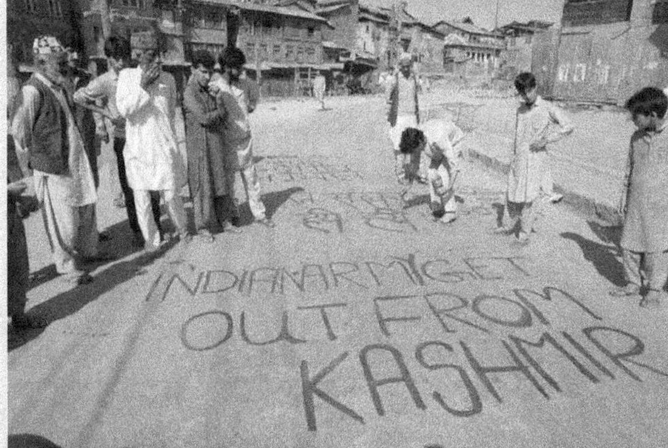

Heavy handed tactics by the Indian security forces – cause more widespread riots.

Burhan Wani was the commander of a Kashmiri militant group Hizbul Mujahideen – fighting for their freedom in Indian occupied Kashmir.

Iqdian security forces heavy handed and oppresive tactics on Kashmiri protestors.

Kashmiri protestors in Indian occupied Kashmir

The Kashmiri uprising in Indian occupied Kashmir is gaining popularity amongst the Kashmiri people – who are seeking freedom from Indian security forces oppression. There are over 700,000 Indian troops in Indian occupied Kashmir that are trying to brutally suppress the indigenous nationalist/separatist/freedom movement. Despite India's brutal tactics, the Kashmiri movement is gaining momentum.

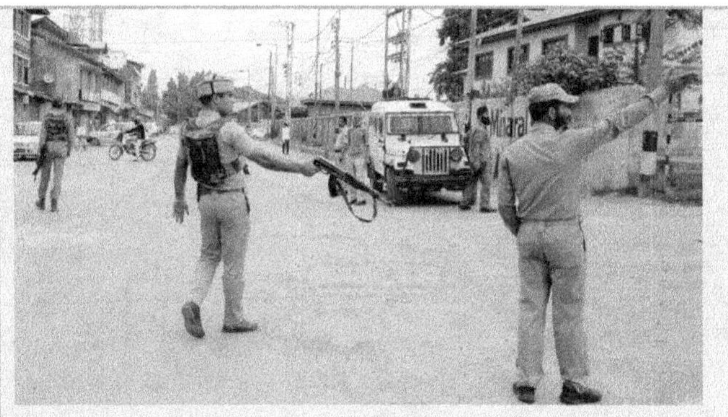

Indian brutality

Militants/freedom fighters in hot pursuit from Indian troops cross the border into Pakistan. 3

Border Skirmish between Pakistan and India – due to hot pursuit of the militants/freedom fighters. Clashes occur. 4

Indian border patrols

Indian troops and Kasmir's rebels fighting against Indian occupation of Kashmir

Pakistani border patrols

Pakistan anti-tank/anti-bunker missile

Kashmir's young rebels

Indian soldiers

Indian and Pakistani soldiers have clashed on numerous occassions on the Line of Control (LOC) in disputed Kashmir. The clashes have resulted in many soldiers and civilians being killed from both sides of the border (primarily due artillery shelling and small arms fire).

Limited border conflict escalates to a major full blown conflict 5

Indian Artillery

Pakistani firepower

Pakistani Multiple Rocket Launchers

3rd major Indo-Pakistan war starts. Indian numerical supremacy takes toll on Pakistani forces. 6

Indian MBT and Artillery

Indian Air Force Strike aircraft

7 Pakistan begins to lose significant forces and territory – India is threatening to cross Pakistan's 'Red' line. Pakistan contemplates in the use of nuclear weapons on Indian troop formations, as a warning. It fires tactical nuclear weapons on Indian military formations – via Nasr battlefield nuclear missile. Watching an Indian response, Pakistan ready to fire its main long-range nuclear capable ballistic missiles.

Tactical nuclear weapons

8 India reacts with firing Nuclear ballistic missile – nuclear conflict erupts. India aims to destroy all known nuclear/launch sites in Pakistan. First major strike – with the plan to destroy all nuclear capability of Pakistani forces.

Indian Prithvi Nuclear ballistic Missile

Indian Agni nuclear capable ballistic missile

Pakistan counter-attacks (second strike capability from its submarines) with SLCM or SLBM in an attempt to destroy Indian forces/cities.

9

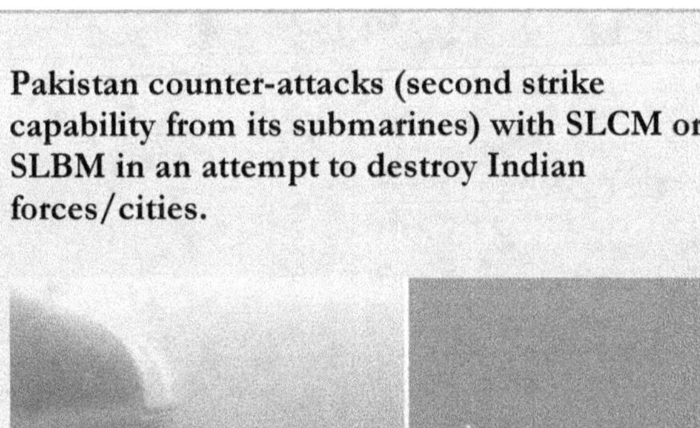

Babur 3 SLCM (Nuclear) – Second strike capability

Indian second strike capability has been initiated from its submarines – aim to destroy remaining Pakistani forces.

10

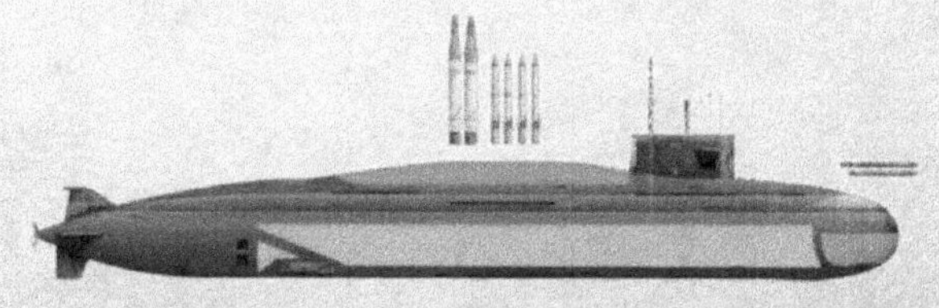

India has a second strike capability that can counter a nuclear first strike successfully.

Pakistan's RAAD Air Launched Cruise Missile (ALCM)

Pakistani and Indian nuclear numbers are roughly 130-150 weapons each – that is approximately up to 300 nuclear weapons to use in the subcontinent. Nuclear holocaust – Armageddon for this region.

In the 1983 film War Games, a nuclear war simulation is accidentally started by a supercomputer designed to take over in event of the cold war spiralling out of control. After evaluating all the possibilities, the computer declares that **"war is a strange game, in which the only winning move – is not to play"**. That advice is possibly truest for Pakistan and India right now. [74]

No winners in a nuclear war???

---

[74] Raghu Raman, Why war with Pakistan—is not an option - https://medium.com/@captraman/why-war-with-pakistan-is-not-an-option-3ccfa25a1529

The unthinkable nuclear nightmare!

Pakistan and India are now on the verge of completing their third leg of the TRIAD (air, land and sea-based nuclear weapon carrying platforms) – with Pakistan's launch of the submarine launched cruise missile (SLCM) it has validated and demonstrated its second strike nuclear capability. India has also demonstrated with its development and testing of the Submarine launched ballistic Missile (SLBM) from its nuclear submarine INS Arihant – giving it a credible nuclear second strike capability. Both countries are continuing to develop and increase the range and sophistication of its missiles.

According to Bharat Kamad (strategic analyst), "The triad becomes effective when you have a submarine operational at all times. In our case, a triad is operational only part of the time-when the Arihant sails out to sea". And further states, " When an Indian SSBN sails out of Visakhapatnam and into the Bay of Bengal, it can virtually disappear for months, remaining underwater, its endurance limited only by the endurance of its crew, communicating only through extremely low frequency (ELF) antennae which it trails in the water. While bombers, mobile missile launchers, missile trains and ground-based launchers can be tracked, nuclear submarines are virtually undetectable. This is what makes them the most precious asset of the nuclear triad".[75]

The Indian nuclear submarine, Arihant is currently being equipped with 12 B-05 SLBMs with a range of 750Km. this is further being improved by the 3,500km K-4 SLBM that is in development. In addition, India is planning for further tests of the K-5 SLBM with an estimated range of over 5,000km (the 'K' series of missiles are named after former president APJ Abdul Kalam).[76]

Pakistan continues to improve its second strike capability to deter any indian aggression – it has successfully tested the 'Babur 3' submarine launched cruise missile (SLCM) and the meduim range, Ababeel (MIRV) ballistic missile that is capable of carrying multiple warheads. The SLCM Babur missile has a range of 280 miles and is thought to be equipped with stealth technologies that will allow it to evade Indian radar and ballistic missile defense systems. The 'Ababeel' missile has a reported range of 1,367 miles and is able to carry multiple nuclear warheads with the assistance of Multiple Independent Re-entry Vehicle technology.[77]

Pakistan's current range of Babur 3 SLCM and Ababeel MIRV ballistic missile – it is assessed that Pakistan will continue to extend the range and sophistication of these missiles in due course.[78]

[75] India Today magazine: A peek into India's top secret and costliest defence project, nuclear submarines - https://www.indiatoday.in/magazine/the-big-story/story/20171218-india-ballistic-missile-submarine-k-6-submarine-launched-drdo-1102085-2017-12-10

[76] Ibid

[77] Pakistan Improves Second Strike Capability With First Successful Submarine Ballistic Missile Launch - http://www.phcintelligencer.com/2017/03/10/pakistans-second-chance/

[78] Pakistan Improves Second Strike Capability With First Successful Submarine Ballistic Missile Launch - http://www.phcintelligencer.com/2017/03/10/pakistans-second-chance/

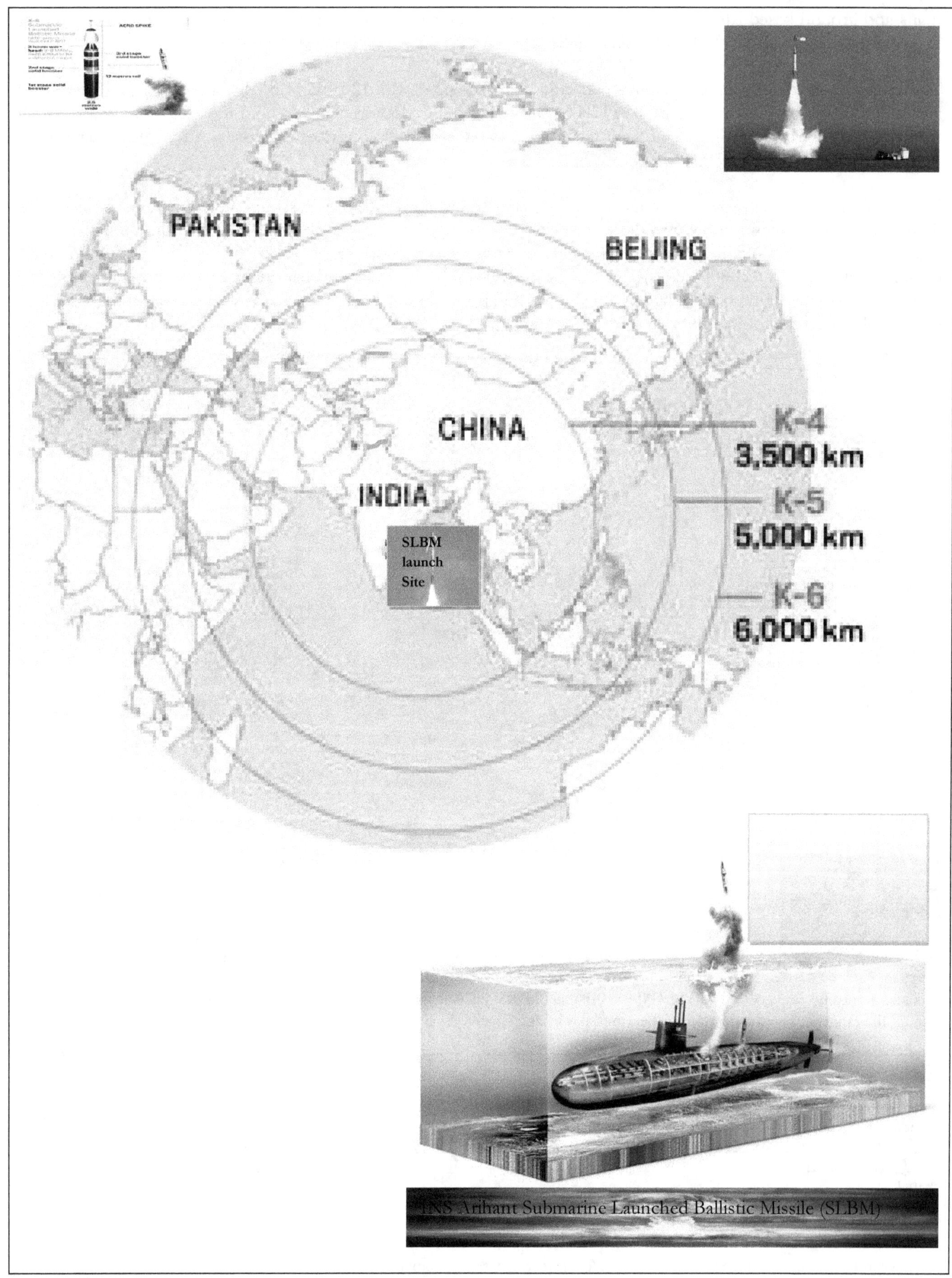

INS Arihant Submarine Launched Ballistic Missile (SLBM)

Now both India and Pakistan have the assured capability of destroying each other – Mutaual Assured Destruction has come to South Asia. This is the reason that it becomes imperative for both nations to amicably address their issues and attempt to resolve it, before any hawkish government from either side decides to start thinking of the unthinkable – nuclear war. The current fundamentalist Indian BJP government of Prime Minister modie and its backing from groups such as the RSS (Indian Fascists whose views are similar to Nazi Germany of the past) – could use heavy handed tactics in Indian security issues and attempt to blame the Pakistani government for their failures (possible false flag operations) could lead to a horendous nuclear war within the subcontinent and this will have global ramifications.

Pakistan Navy Khalid Class (Agosta) submarine on patrol

Indian aircraft carrier with Mig-29 Fulcrum multi-role combat aircraft[79]

---

[79] India eyes military expansion; Sitharaman to spend Diwali with soldiers in Andaman tri-service command - http://www.civilsdaily.com/story/defence-sector/

Chapter 4: The Impact of an Indo-Pakistan Nuclear War

The Impact of an Indo-Pakistan Nuclear War

India and Pakistan are estimated to have nuclear weapons between 130-150 nuclear warheads each. An analysis of the consequences of a nuclear war was undertaken by the Natural Resources defense Council (NRDC) on two given scenarios of using 10 Hiroshima-sized explosions without any fallout and 24 nuclear explosions with massive radioactive fallout. 15 kiloton yield (1 kiloton is equivalent to 1,000 tons of TNT) was the power on the bomb dropped on Hiroshima, Japan by the united states of America. For the purpose of this scenario, it is assumed that both India and Pakistan possess 15 kiloton yield of the Hiroshima weapon.[80]

Scenario 1: 10 Bombs on 10 South Asian Cities

Casualty data from the Hiroshima bomb to estimate what would happen if bombs exploded over 10 large South Asian cities was used: 5 in India and 5 in Pakistan. 10 nuclear weapons would kill 3 to 4 times more people per bomb than in Japan because of the higher urban densities in Indian and Pakistani cities. The 15-kiloton yield of the Hiroshima equivalent weapon was based on the following:[81]

- Deaths and severe injuries experienced at Hiroshima were mainly a function of how far people were from ground zero.
- Factors included whether people were in buildings or outdoors,
- The structural characteristics of the buildings themselves,
- The age and health of the victims at the time of the attack.
- The closer to ground zero, the higher fatality rate.
- Further away there were fewer fatalities and larger numbers of injuries.

---

[80] Syed Ali Abbas Zaidi's Blog, Consequences of India-Pakistan Nuclear War -
https://plastictearz.wordpress.com/2010/02/09/consequences-of-india-pakistan-nuclear-war/

[81] Ibid

Estimated nuclear casualties for attacks on 10 large Indian and Pakistani cities

City Name	Total Population Within 5 Kilometers of Ground Zero	Number of Persons Killed	Number of Persons Severely Injured	Number of Persons Slightly Injured
		India		
Bangalore	3,077,937	314,978	175,136	411,336
Bombay	3,143,284	477,713	228,648	476,633
Calcutta	3,520,344	357,202	198,218	466,336
Madras	3,252,628	364,291	196,226	448,948
New Delhi	1,638,744	176,518	94,231	217,853
Total India	14,632,937	1,690,702	892,459	2,021,106
		Pakistan		
Faisalabad	2,376,478	336,239	174,351	373,967
Islamabad	798,583	154,067	66,744	129,935
Karachi	1,962,458	239,643	126,810	283,290
Lahore	2,682,092	258,139	149,649	354,095
Rawalpindi	1,589,828	183,791	96,846	220,585
Total Pakistan	9,409,439	1,171,879	614,400	1,361,872
		India and Pakistan		
Total	24,042,376	2,862,581	1,506,859	3,382,978

Scenario 2: 24 Ground Bursts

In this scenario 24 nuclear explosions are detonated on the ground (unlike Hiroshima airburst, which resulted in great amounts of lethal radioactive fallout). It is assumed that a dozen 25 kiloton warheads would be detonated each in India and Pakistan. The results are as follows:[82]

15 Indian and Pakistani cities attacked with 24 nuclear warheads

Country	City	City Population	Number of Attacking Bombs
Pakistan	Islamabad (national capital)	100-250 thousand	1
Pakistan	Karachi (provincial capital)	> 5 million	3
Pakistan	Lahore (provincial capital)	1-5 million	2
Pakistan	Peshawar (provincial capital)	0.5-1 million	1
Pakistan	Quetta (provincial capital)	250-500 thousand	1
Pakistan	Faisalabad	1-5 million	2
Pakistan	Hyderabad	0.5-1 million	1
Pakistan	Rawalpindi	0.5-1 million	1
India	New Dehli (national capital)	250-500 thousand	1

---

[82] Syed Ali Abbas Zaidi's Blog, Consequences of India-Pakistan Nuclear War -
https://plastictearz.wordpress.com/2010/02/09/consequences-of-india-pakistan-nuclear-war/

India	Bombay (provincial capital)	> 5 million	3
India	Delhi (provincial capital)	> 5 million	3
India	Jaipur (provincial capital)	1-5 million	2
India	Bhopal (provincial capital)	1-5 million	1
India	Ahmadabad	1-5 million	1
India	Pune	1-5 million	1

The NRDC results are as follows:

- 22.1 million people in India and Pakistan would be exposed to lethal radiation in the first two days after the attack.

- Another 8 million people would receive a severe radiation, causing severe radiation sickness and potentially death, especially for the very young, old or infirm.

- Approximately 30 million people would be threatened by the fallout from the attack, roughly divided between the two countries.

- Besides fallout, blast and fire would cause substantial destruction within roughly a mile-and-a-half of the bomb craters. NRDC estimates that 8.1 million people live within this radius of destruction.[83]

According to another estimate (2013 research paper by the International Physicians for the Prevention of Nuclear War), 21 million people will be killed instantly with significant environmental damage on a global scale. It states, **"If India and Pakistan fought a war detonating 100 nuclear warheads (around half of their combined arsenal), each equivalent to a 15-kiloton Hiroshima bomb, more than 21 million people will be directly killed, about half the world's protective ozone layer would be destroyed, and a "nuclear winter" would cripple the monsoons and agriculture worldwide. An additional two billion people worldwide would face risks of severe starvation due to the climatic effects of the nuclear war".[84]**

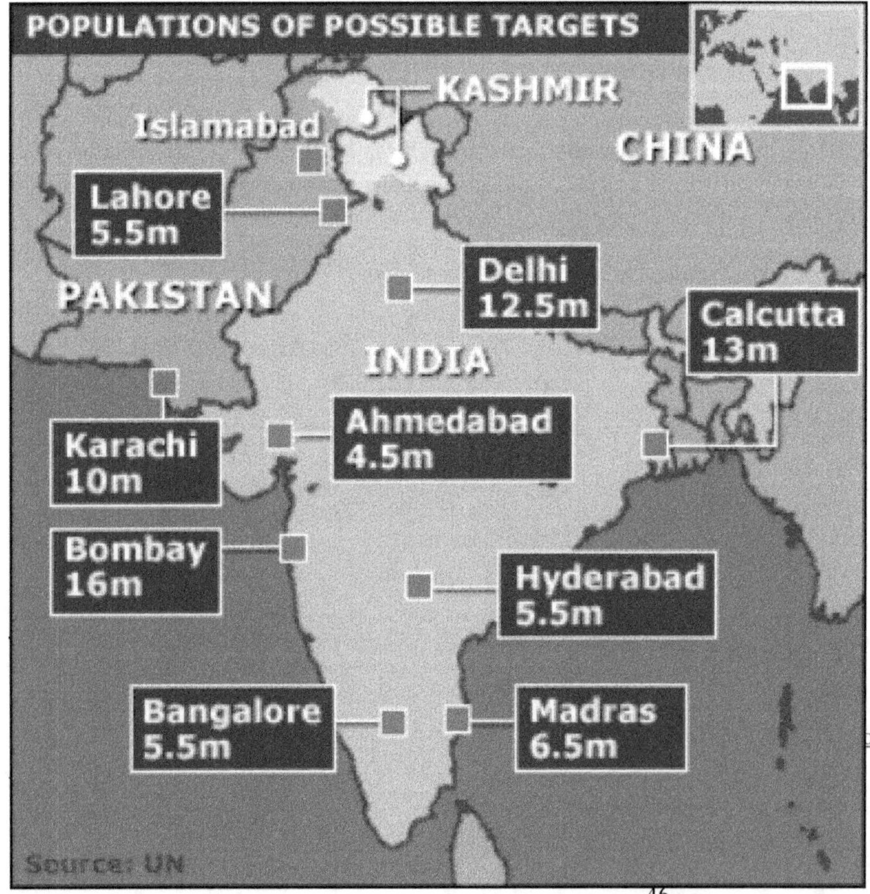

As can been seen that a nuclear exchange between India and Pakistan would bring horendous loss of lives with devasting environmental consequences. A possible nuclear winter and the destruction of many lives across the globe. In addition it would bring economic recession and disruption of the global economic trade.[85]

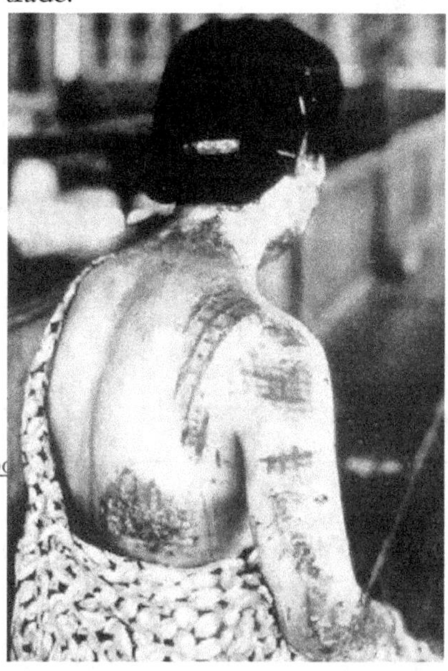

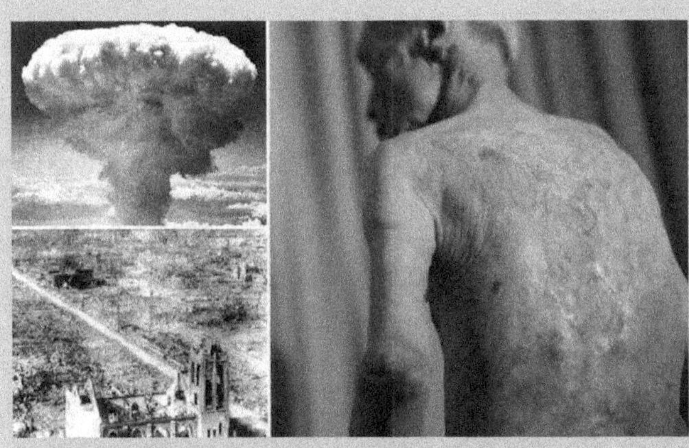

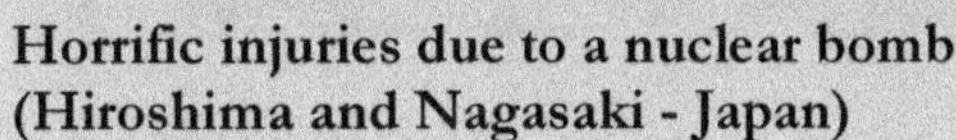

Horrific injuries due to a nuclear bomb
(Hiroshima and Nagasaki - Japan)

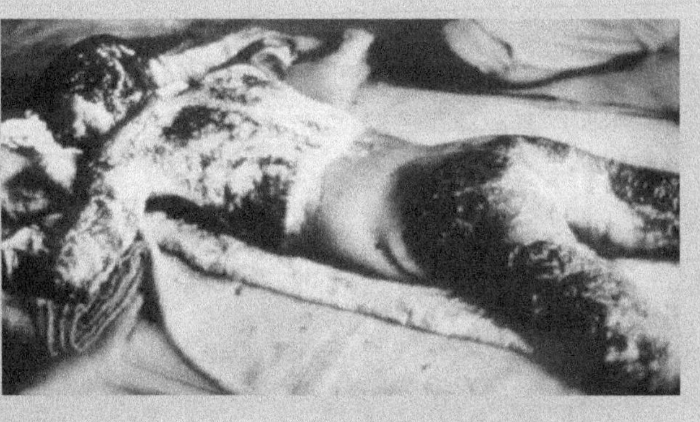

Horrific injuries caused by a nuclear bomb

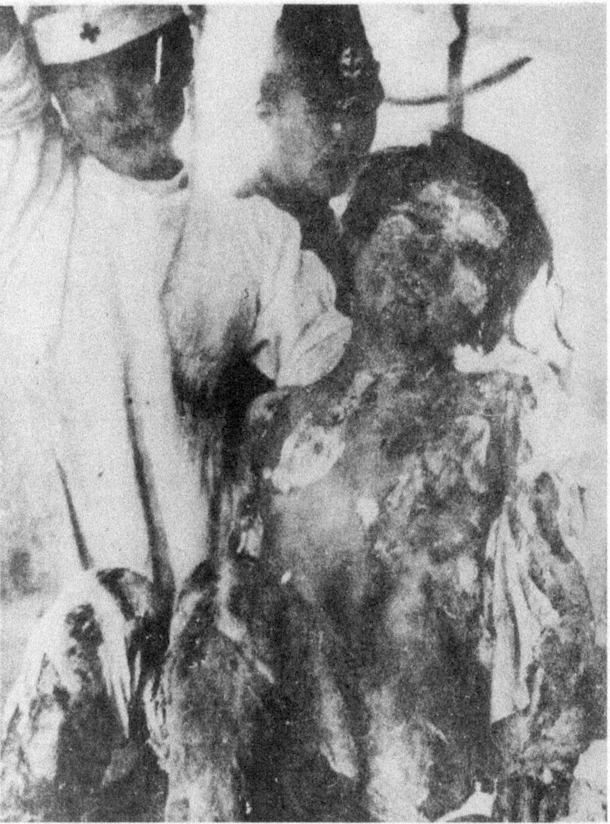

Horrific injuries due to a nuclear bomb (Hiroshima and
Nagasaki - Japan)

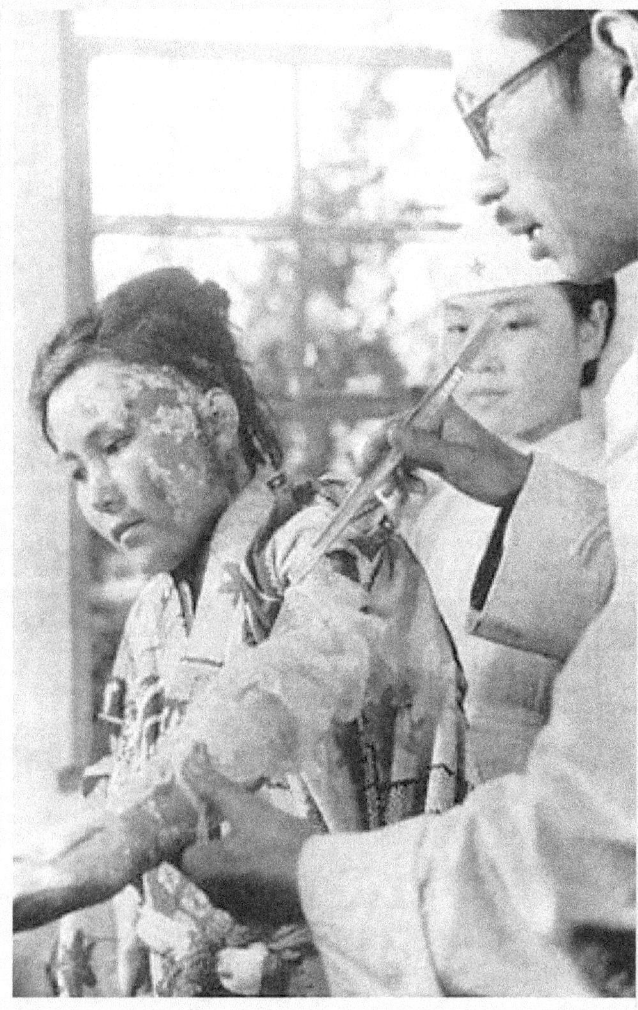

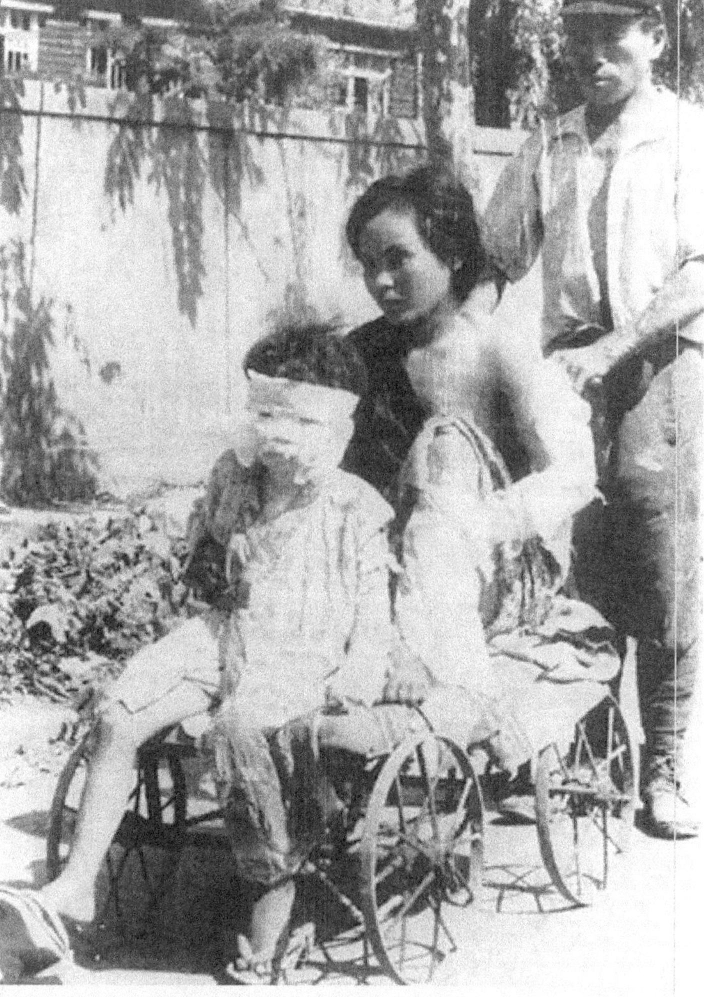

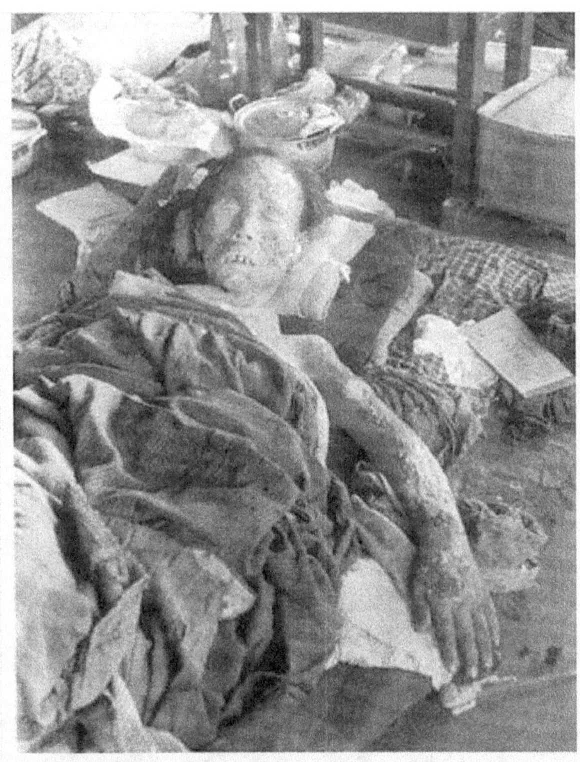

Nuclear devastation caused by the nuclear bombs dropped by the USA on Japan - Hiroshima and Nagasaki cities were destroyed with horendous injuries and casualties.

The impact on Indo-Pakistan nuclear war is unthinkable – but in reality it can easily be triggered by any miscalculation from either side. There are enough issues on the boil in this part of the world and it would not take too long for either side to misconstrue each others intentions – which could lead to a nuclear holocaust.

India successfully test-fires nuclear capable Prithvi-II

Chapter 5: The Military Imbalance

Indian Main Battle Tank (MBT)

Indo-Pakistan Military Imbalance

Pakistan and India have fought three major wars and various other confrontations since 1947. With Pakistan possessing only one-fourth of the land mass and less than one-sixth of the population of India, there are real concerns amongst Pakistani strategists that India could dismember their country in much the same way as in the 1971 war (a 'soft spot' would be through the Sindh province, separating the capital at Islamabad from the economic centre at Karachi) and defeat Pakistan's conventional forces in about two weeks.[86]

Pakistani strategies believe India's large army is well out of proportion to her defence needs. In particular, India's drive to modernise its army with well-equipped air and naval components, has significantly enhanced its power projection capabilities.[87] Relationship with China had, until recently, improved considerably. India's other neighbours are considered to be insignificant to pose any real threat. India's 20 year modernisation drive has enabled it to acquire a nuclear and ballistic missile capability, as well as improve its conventional military might. It has also greatly enhanced its strategic surveillance and reconnaissance abilities, with its own satellite with highly accurate imagery.[88] India's quest for great power status rather than national security is apparently uppermost in the minds of her politicians. We will look briefly at this conventional military capability, as well as that of Pakistan.

India has fought 3 major wars with Pakistan, and two mini-wars in the Siachin Glacier (Kashmir),[89] on the highest

---

[86]JDW, Pakistan's time for Reassessment, 1988, Pg9
[87] 2.) Anthony H. Cordesman, Western Strategic Interests and the India-Pakistan Military Balance, Ian Allan Ltd, 1988, Pg83
[88] 3.) India Today, India is now a Nuclear Weapons State, Living Media India Ltd, 1998, Pg23
[89] JDW, Fighting on the Roof of the World, 1998, Pg27

battlefield of the world and also fought in Kargil (Kashmir). Recently, it has publicly demonstrated its designs on globally projecting its power. On at least two occasions, (in 1987 during India's Brasstacks' military exercise, and in the uprising in Kashmir in 1990), Kargil Mini-war in 1999, Pakistan and India have come close to full-scale military conflict.[90]

Of particular concern for Pakistan is the open-source estimates that India has now manufactured between 130 nuclear devices.[91] In addition, the recent BJP government has been engaged in an open display of 'sabre-rattling' against Pakistan. It has openly declared its intention to 'take back' Pakistan-held Kashmir, as well as targeting of Pakistani cities, infrastructure, industries and defence installations by the Indian Air Force (IAF), and the development of new missile systems. These include the short range ballistic missile (SRBM) Prithvi and the intermediate range ballistic missile (IRBM) Agni; two surface to air missiles (SAM), the Trishul and the Akash; and also an anti-tank guided missile (ATGM), the Nag.[92] It has further tested Submarine Launched Ballistic Missiles from the Indian Submarine Arihant and has tested the Agni 5 Intercontinental Ballistic Missile (ICBM) with over 5,000 km range.

The Prithvi missile (150-350 km) and the development of the Agni IRBM (1500-2500 km) and other longer range series of Indian ballistic missiles provide India with the capability of targeting major Pakistani cities.[93] The plans to develop and deploy these missiles are seen by Pakistan as a proof of India's hostile designs. In addition, the procurement of 250 state-of-the-art Su-30MKI Flanker multi-role strike aircraft gives more punch to the Indian offensive capabilities on land and in the air, seriously undermining Pakistan's immediate and perceived security.[94]

India also has indigenous defence production programmes, including the manufacture of Soviet designed Mig-27 and British 'Jaguar' attack aircraft's the development of its own jet fighter that was initially called the light combat aircraft (LCA) is now known as Tejas and also an airborne warning and control (AWACS) aircraft. T-90/T-72 tanks, the design and manufacture of the 'Arjun' main battle tank (MBT), modern destroyers; frigates, missile boats, radar, command and communication systems and a full range of missiles and munitions are also in or past the development stages.[95]

India is also purchasing various types of equipment from abroad, such as the planned purchase of over 1025+ advanced Russian T-90S Tanks with licenced production.[96] In addition, it is also planning to purchase over 600 self-propelled Howitzers for the Army,[97] over 100 combat capable trainers for the airforce,[98] the Admiral Gorshkov aircraft carrier from Russia. Its massive military build-up in the past two decades has been fully supported by India's indigenous defence manufacturing industries, enabling India to sustain a full scale conventional military conflict for a longer period if the need arose.[99]

Defence Budget and Arms Purchases

The India and Pakistan dispute has encouraged military modernisation in the region- the two countries are spending more on their military forces, making this part of the world the one region where military expenditure has been rising since the end of the Cold War. In the period from 1987-96 the two countries military expenditure had amounted to a massive $108.92 billion.[100] Since then it has increased massively, India alone intends to spend over $200 billion on defence systems by 2022.[101] The South Asian share of world military expenditure has increased over the past number

---

[90] India Today, Games of Brinkmanship, 1987, Pg8
[91] JDW, Trials Provide Data for Range of Weapons Yields, 1998, Pg3
[92] JDW, Asia's Missile Race Hots Up, 1994, Pg20
[93] Ibid
[94] JDW, IAF Follows up on SU-30 Offer, 1994, Pg4
[95] Impact International, Delhi Expands its Strategic Swath, News & Media Ltd, 1996, Pg24
[96] JDW, India Budget May Affect Modernisation, 1998, Pg29
[97] JDW, India's Search for a New SPG, 1994, Pg45
[98] Flight International, Airforces of the World Directory, Marketforce Ltd, 1998, Pg68
[99] JDW, Indian Budget Fall May Affect Modernisation, 1998, Pg29
[100] Stockholm International Peace Research Institute (SIPRI), World Military Expenditure Prices 1987-96, Oxford University Press, 1997, Pg197
[101] India to spend $200 bn on defence systems by 2022 - https://www.hindustantimes.com/delhi-news/india-to-spend-200-bn-on-defence-systems-by-2022/story-K2MzbLCRGranHRyrsii5SJ.html

of years, defence expenditures in 2017 amounted to some \$62.22 billion (\$52.5 billion for India and \$9.72 billion Pakistan) and this was projected to rise every year.[102] As a percentage of their Gross Domestic Product (GDP), Pakistan spends a lot more on military expenditure as a percentage of its GDP, for instance in the period from 1987-96 it spent an average of 7.5% of its GDP. In contrast India spent an average of 2.8% of its GDP from the 1987-96 period. However this is because the Indian economy is growing at a better rate than Pakistan.[103]

According to Stockholm International Peace Research Institute (SIPRI) in 2015 - India spent around 2.3 % of its GDP on military, which was \$51.3 billion and Pakistan spent 3.4% of their GDP on military, which is \$9.5 billion.[104]

Year (SIPRI)	India		Pakistan	
	GDP	Amount in USD	GDP	Amount in USD
2005	2.8%	35,718	3.7%	7,032
2006	2.5%	36,151	3.4%	7,081
2007	2.3%	41,003	3.1%	6,676
2008	2.6%	48,277	3.1%	6,879
2009	2.9%	48,470	3.1%	7,134
2010	2.7%	48,940	3.1%	7,520
2011	2.6%	48,766	3.3%	7,975
2012	2.5%	48,406	3.2%	8,238
2013	2.4%	50,914	3.3%	8,655
2014	2.5%	51,116	3.3%	9,248
2015	2.3%	51,257	3.4%	9,510

Data source SIPRI

Pakistan spends a high proportion of its GDP on military expenditure, to balance Indian military superiority. However, in real terms India spends on average nearly three times more on military expenditure than Pakistan does. For example, in 1998, Indian expenditure was \$9.9bn compared to Pakistan's \$3.2bn.[105] This equates to just over three times more than Pakistan spends, thereby encouraging Pakistan to spend a higher proportion of its GDP to try to minimally match India's military capabilities. India spent nearly four times more on military expenditure in 2017. India had become largest arms importer from 1950-2017, importing a massive \$119.89 billion worth of weapons.

---

[102] International Institute for Strategic Studies (IISS), Military Balance 1998-99, Oxford University Press, 1998, Pg155-160
[103] SIPRI 1997, op cit:203
[104] Freya Dasgupta (2016) Who Spends More On Their Military, India Or Pakistan? - https://www.outlookindia.com/blog/story/who-spends-more-on-their-military-india-or-pakistan/3837

[105] IISS, op cit:155-160

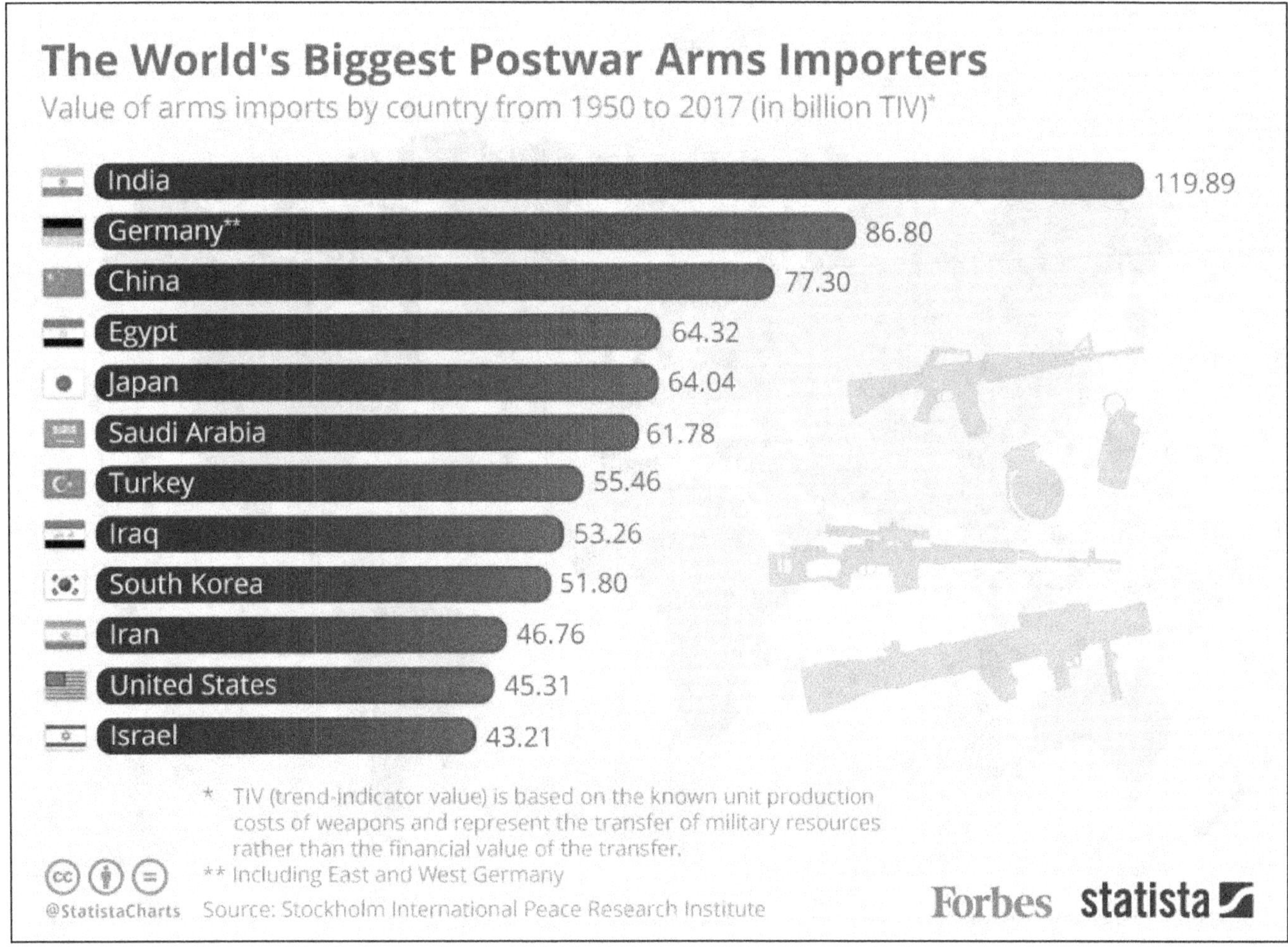

The World's Biggest Arms Importers Since 1950[106]

India's military superiority over Pakistan becomes even clearer as one examines the details of the military balance.

The Balance of Land Forces

According to the International Institute for Strategic Studies (The Military Balance 2018), quantitative differences in the number of men and weapons gave the following ratios between India and Pakistan. India enjoys an over two-to-one advantage in army personnel (1,200,000 to 560,000).[107] The superiority further increases to approximately 5.6 to 1 if paramilitary personnel are taken into account (over 1,585,950 million to almost 282,000). India's superiority in army manpower is matched by its overall advantage over Pakistan in nearly all categories of ground combat equipment. In main battle tanks (MBT), the Indian advantage is approximately 1.5 to one (4,197 to 2,737), in mechanised infantry vehicles (APCs/AIFV/Recce) approximately 1.7 to one (2,836 to 1,715), in artillery 2.2 to one (9,684 to 4,472), and in multi-role helicopters 3.6 to one (787 to 216). In only one area, attack helicopters, does Pakistan enjoy an advantage which is 2.2 to one (42 to 19).[108]

---

[106] The World's Biggest Arms Importers Since 1950 - https://www.forbes.com/sites/niallmccarthy/2018/03/12/the-worlds-biggest-post-war-arms-importers-infographic/#32e3fa118e34

[107] Ibid
[108] Ibid

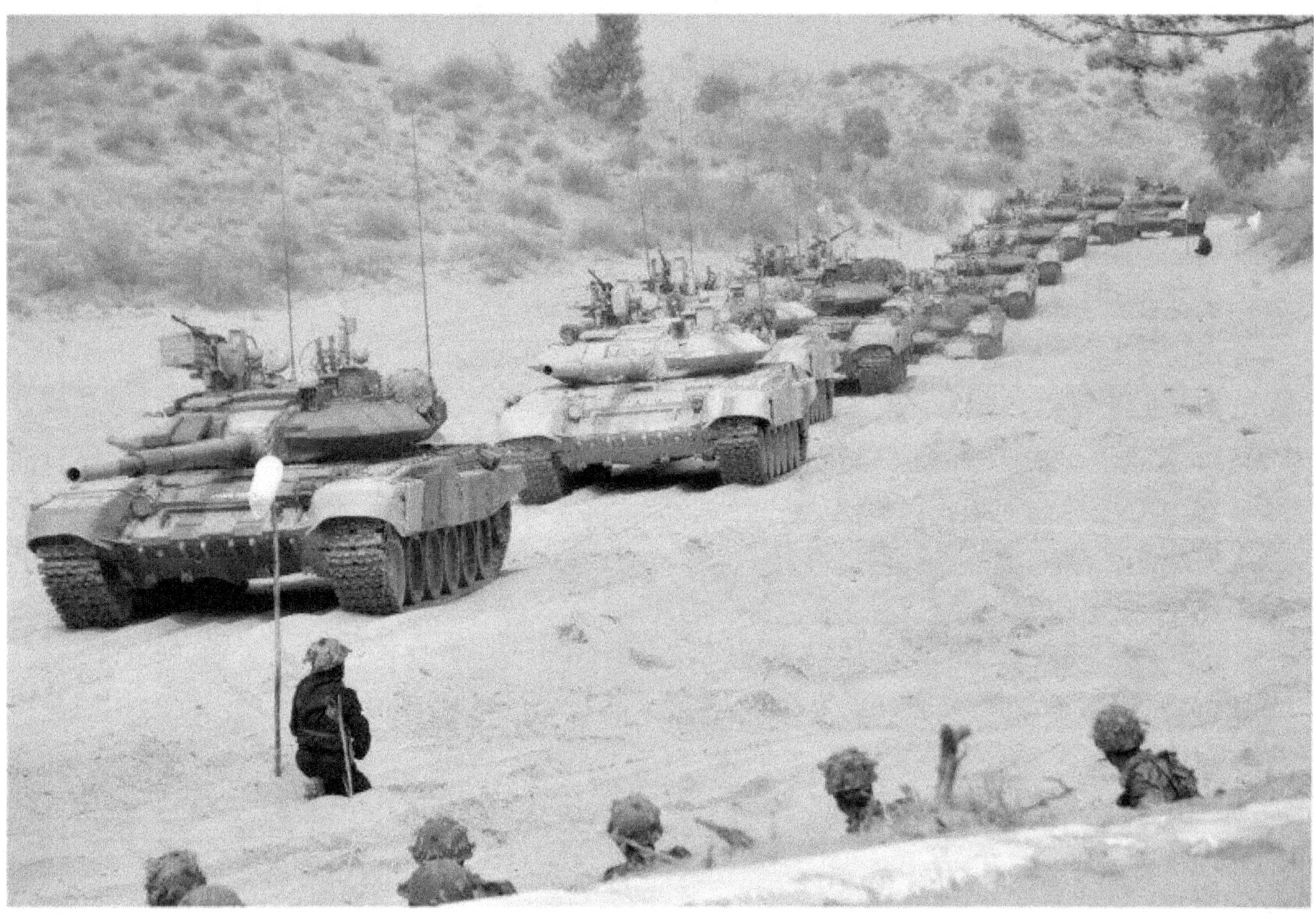

Cold Start': India deploys hundreds of Russian-made battle tanks along Pakistan border[109]

The ratios cited above are based on the total number of each type of equipment in the respective inventories. They do not take into account the qualitative differences of their ground force equipment. Thus, in addition to its obvious quantitative advantage, India also enjoys a qualitative advantage in most categories of equipment as well.

All in all, India maintains a large army consisting of well over 1.2 million men, supported by a large reserve force consisting of 960,000 men. The standing army is distributed into three armoured divisions, six semi-armoured divisions (RAPID), 35 infantry and mountain divisions, fifteen independent brigades.[110] Pakistan sees this large military build-up as Pakistan-specific. They argue that the mechanised and armoured forces, with a total of 4,197 tanks, cannot be used against the island of Sri Lanka, nor in the soggy terrain of Bangladesh. They are also not needed in the mountains of tiny Nepal and cannot cross the mighty Himalayan mountain ranges towards China, Pakistan, clearly, is the target.[111]

The Balance of Air Forces

The recent Gulf War and also the war in Kosova (NATO's air war) has shown that the outcome of any future conflict will rest heavily on control of the skies and the ability to deny the enemy of the same. The Indian Air Force (IAF) is the 4th largest in the world and growing rapidly. It justifies its size by pointing to the Chinese PLAAF (Peoples

---

[109] 'Cold Start': India deploys hundreds of Russian-made battle tanks along Pakistan border -https://en.dailypakistan.com.pk/headline/cold-start-india-deploys-hundreds-of-russian-made-battle-tanks-along-pakistan-border/

[110] Ibid

[111] The News International, Armed to the Teeth, Jang Publishers Ltd, 1998, Pg10

Liberation Army Air Force).[112]

In comparison to Pakistan Air force, Indian again enjoys a sizeable advantage in this field too. In personnel strength, it has almost a 1.8 to 1 advantage (127,200 to 70,000). In terms of operational units, the Indian Air Force (IAF) has a 3.6 to one edge in ground attack fighter squadrons (29 to 8), two to one in air-defence fighter squadrons this time in Pakistan's adavantage (6 to 3), and two to one in reconnaissance squadrons (2 to 1). In terms of equipment, the IAF has a better than 2 to 1 advantage in jet combat aircraft (849 to 425) and over 6.9 to one in transports (241 to 35).[113]

PAF F-16 Falcon combat aircraft dropping bombs

An important area for comparison is the number of sophisticated fighter in each air force. For the Pakistan Air force (PAF), its most capable aircraft include the F-16 (76), the JF-17 Thunder (85), the Mirage 3 (82) and the Mirage 5 (89) of which there are a total of 332. In comparison, the IAF has a better than 1.6 to one advantage with total of 546 aircraft that could be considered state-of-the-art including Mirage 2000s (50), Jaguars (117), Mig-27s (65), Mig-29s (62), LCA Tejas (2), and the SU-30MK (250).[114]

While the IAF has a numerical advantage, it also has a qualitative advantage over the Pakistan Air force, which it will retain under any currently foreseeable conditions. Qualitatively, the IAF must also be considered one of the best-equipped services in the World. The majority of India's combat aircraft are comparable to front-line NATO/WTP aircraft. It is also virtually certain that the Indian advantage in the air will continue to contribute far more support of the Indian Army than the PAF can contribute to the support of the Pakistan Army.[115]

It is also important to note that the F-16A/Cs and other aircraft in the PAF will not face a Mig-21 or Mig-23 threat in the late 2018s. They will face an Indian threat equipped with the state-of-the-art Russian fighters like the SU-30MKI and the MIG 29, French fighters like the Mirage 2000, and a wide range of new Western/Russian systems in Indian forces.[116] The Indian Air Force has also ordered the sophisticated French Rafael multi-role combat aircraft – these aircrafts would poise extra threats to the PAF.

All in all, among its ranks the IAF contains Mirage 2000H aircraft, Mig-27 attack aircraft, Mig-29 interceptors and Anglo-French Jaguar deep-strike attack aircraft. The bombers and a large transport fleet is in addition. For their protection there are 30 surface-to-air missile squadrons. Also existing fleets of 125 Mig-21 bis and 65 Mig-27s are being updated. The development of India's Light Combat Aircraft (LCA) has been completed and orders have been made – the IAF plans to induct up to 324 LCA Tejas[117] multi-role combat aircraft.[118]

Over and above this, India has purchased 250 modern Russian built state of the art SU-30MK force-multiplier multi-role fighter aircraft. Especially with the recent acquisition of the SU-30MKIs, the IAF has at least on paper, tremendously improved its qualitative standing. With the force listed above, the IAF is capable of using the latest 'smart' weaponry, stand-off weapons, extremely long range air-to-air missiles such as the AA-10 Alamo and countless

---

[112] JDW, Country Survey-India, 1990, Pg1023

[113] IISS, op cit:155-160

[114] Ibid

[115] Cordesman, op cit:132

[116] Cordesman, op cit:182

[117] IAF commits to 324 Tejas fighters, provided a good Mark-II jet is delivered - https://timesofindia.indiatimes.com/india/iaf-commits-to-324-tejas-fighters-provided-a-good-mark-2-jet-is-delivered/articleshow/63306776.cms

[118] Flight International, op cit:68

other lethal stores. It is also capable of delivering nuclear weapons deep inside Pakistani territory.[119]

India is also steadily improving the quality of its air weaponry and is obtaining some of the latest and most capable Russian air-to-air and air-to-ground munitions. Qualitative enhancements in IAF aircraft include 'BVR' or Beyond Visual Range capability. This allows a fighter pilot to track, lock and destroy a target while it is far away. The IAF has recently acquired AA-10 Alamo missiles which will allow such attacks to be made against Pakistani aircraft at a range of more than 100km. This greatly reduces the chances of aerial combat coming down to dogfights, where pilot's skill is the deciding factor and an area in which the Pakistan Air Force has the qualitative edge. All SU-30MKIs and Mig-29s have BVR capability whereas the PAF had limited capability. In addition, the longest-range air-to-air missiles in the Pakistan Air Force is the AIM-7 Sparrow which has barely 1/3rd the range of an Alamo.[120] For the PAF things had gradually improved when a large amount of US Amraam BVR missiles were ordered, In addition the Chinese SD-10 BVR missile has been ordered for its JF-17 Thunder multi-role combat aircraft. This gives the PAF the same advantage as the IAF have had with their BVR missiles.

Furthermore, the IAF has also taken due note of the electronic spectrum which had successfully paralysed Iraqi air defences and command communications during the Gulf War. India has developed the capability to use EW technology to cripple command and communications of adversary's Army, Navy and Air Force. IAF has acquired a wide range of BVR munitions. Such capabilities have greatly enhanced the offensive and defensive capabilities of the IAF.[121]

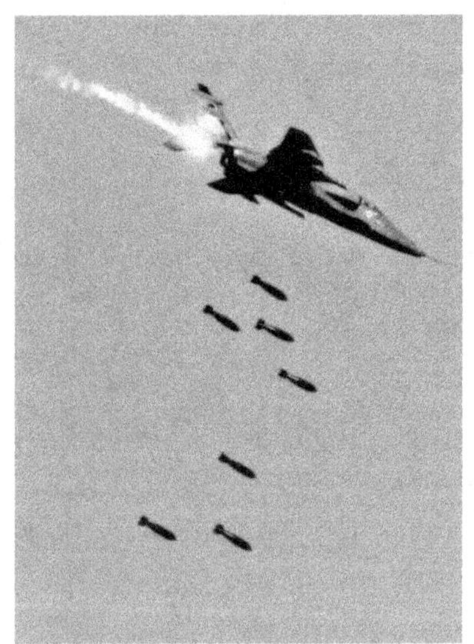

IAF Jaguar attack aircraft dropping its bombs

In contrast to the IAF, the Pakistan Air force (PAF) is much smaller, and is also far less modern. The PAF's 425 combat aircraft now include only 76 sophisticated F-16s and 85 JF-17 Thunder combat aircrafts. Its only other comparatively modern fighters are 171 last-generation Mirage 3/5s. The majority of the PAF consists of Chinese combat aircraft such as the F-7P/PG interceptors; these are Chinese variants of the old Russian Mig-21 (mid-aircraft 1960s vintage). It has also purchased updated Chinese F-7M (MIG-21) fighters. These aircrafts are capable of combat close to Pakistan's borders, but lack the capability to strike deep into Indian territory.[122]

In view of the limited strategic depth of the country, Pakistani air bases are located within striking range of Indian aircraft. If they choose, the Indians can base their aircraft deep into their own territory, but still have the range to reach the border area where the battle will likely occur. The PAF badly needs to replace its F-7P/PG and some of its older Mirage combat aircraft, most of which are obsolete or obsolescent and lack modern avionics, weaponry and performance capability. It is trying to solve this problem by the purchase and modification of large numbers of its co-developed Chinese and Pakistani fighter – the JF-17 Thunder multi-role combat aircraft.[123] It is thought that the PAF could be ordering between 250–300 JF-17 Thunder aircraft in total, which would give a significant boost to the PAF in inducting modern sophisticated aircraft.

Overall, since 1989, the PAF has shrunk due to the non-procurement of aircraft and weapons, and the air power imbalance, if allowed to continue, will threaten its national security beyond repair. The American Pressler Amendment has denied the duly paid-for F-16 fighters (71 had been ordered) and access to other US-made fighter, radars or missiles.[124] Furthermore, Pakistan's Chief of the Air Staff recently stated that, Air power will be decisive factor in any future conflict. Future wars will start with air power, and defeat and victory will be decided when either side concedes defeat in the air.[125]

---

[119] Brassey's, World Aircraft & Systems Directory, Brassey's Ltd, 1996, Pg92
[120] India Today, Future Fire, 1998, Pg22
[121] Ibid
[122] Cordesman, op cit:133
[123] Ibid
[124] JDW, A Loss of Momentum, 1997, Pg45
[125] Ibid

The Balance of Naval Forces

As is the case with air and ground forces, India's Navy enjoys numeric as well as qualitative superiority over Pakistan. India has conducted large-scale modernisation and expansion programmes to improve its ability to exercise sea control and denial and to ensure security of its coastline and island territories against any major naval power. In the 1971 Indo-Pakistani war, the Indian Navy was able to carry out a successful sea blockade of Pakistan's only major port.[126]

Indian Navy Aircraft Carrier with Mig-29 Combat aircraft

Today, India has a large Navy, which continues to grow. At present, it has one aircraft carriers, 14 submarines, 14 missile destroyers, 13 frigates, 108 missile boats and corvettes, supported by fighter and long range reconnaissance aircraft and 83 armed helicopters. It has over a 17 landing craft with an amphibious list capability of 1,200 strong marine force with their arms and equipment. This large force poses a potent threat to Pakistan and the other nearby states of the Indian Ocean.[127]

In contrast, Pakistan has no aircraft carriers, it only has 8 submarines, 0 missiles destroyers, 10 frigates, 17 missile boats and corvettes, supported by 7 medium range maritime patrol aircraft and 12 armed helicopters. It has 1,200 strong marine force with their arms and equipment. This small force does not pose a potent threat to India.

In terms of personnel, the Indian advantage is approximately 2.5 to one (58,350 to 23,800). In major surface combatants, India enjoys a better than 2.8 to one advantage (28 to 10). Of particular note is the fact that India has one aircraft carrier, whereas Pakistan has none. The Indian Navy also enjoys a 1.8 to one advantage in submarines (14 to 8) and a better than 6.9 to one edge in maritime patrol aircraft (48 to 7).[128]

On the whole, the Indian Navy is a formidable force when compared with other navies in the area. No local navy, including the Pakistani Navy, is able to compete on the open seas with the Indian Navy. Pakistan's naval units (surface, combatants, submarines, naval aircraft), cannot prevent India from attacking Pakistan's coastline. Only the acquisition of the AM-39 Exocet air-to-surface missile (ASM) for the Naval Air Arm, and the Harpoon surface-to-surface missile (SSM) for surface combatants, gives Pakistan even a limited capability to inflict losses on Indian vessels operating in its territorial waters. All in all, the Pakistani Navy is a small force capable of defending its own coastal waters. In combination with 'Exocet' armed- Mirages, the Pakistani Navy (PN) might be able to keep the Indian Navy away from the port of Karachi, and could make an amphibious operation costly, but it is no match for the Indian Navy away from the Pakistani coast.[129] Pakistan has also ordered new sophisticated long range anti-ship missiles from China and has currently tested its own missiles – these should give the PN the ability to inflict serious losses to a hostile power.

---

126 Cordesman, op cit:182
127 IISS, op cit:155-160
128 Ibid
129 Cordesman, op cit:182

The following table will show the military imbalance between India and Pakistan.

<u>Pakistan-India Conventional Military Balance 2018</u>

Conventional Military Balance	India	Pakistan
<u>Defence Budgets</u>	Rs3.60tr ($52.5bn)	Rs1.02tr ($9.72bn)
<u>Army</u> **(Total Military Personnel)**	1,200,000 (Active) Reserves 960,000 **Paramilitary forces** 1,585,950 active	560,000 (Active) Reserves 500,000 **Paramilitary forces** 282,000 active
<u>Tanks</u>	4197+ 1,025+ **T-90s** 1,950 **T-72M1 Ajeya,** 122 **Arjun MK.1** (1,100 **various models in store**)	2737+ 21 **Al-Khalid I** 300 **Al-Khalid** (MBT 2000) 320 **T-80UD,** 275+ **T- 85II AP,** 51 **T-54/T-55,** 400 **T-69,** 1,100 **T-59/Al-Zarrar** (270 **M-48A5** in store)
APCs	2,836 (Including **AIFV/ RECCE**)	1,715 **M-113**
Artillery	9,684+ (Including self-propelled artillery) 19 **Mi-25/Mi35 Hind** (Air	4,472 (Including self-propelled artillery) 38 **AH-1F/S Cobra** (Army) 4 **Mi-35M Hind**

Helicopters (Combat)	Force)	
Air Force (Active personnel)	140,000 (Reserves 140,000)	70,000 (Reserves 8,000)
Combat Aircraft 	849 combat capable 250 **Su-30MKI-II** 62 **MIG-29/UB**, 50 **Mirage** 2000H/TH, 117 **Jaguar IS/IT/IM**, 65 **MIG-27ML**, 20 **MIG-23 UB**, 174 **MIG-21BIS** (for **MIG**-21-93 upgrade) **MIG**-21 U/FL/U, 2 **LCA/Tejas** (+**109** Various – not indicated in military balance2018)	425 combat capable 76 F-16 **A/B/C/D**, 93 **F-7P/PG/FT-7 Airguard/Skybolt** (**MIG-21**), 85 **JF-17 Thunder**, 82 **Mirage III B/EP**,OD/R 51(+38) **Mirage V PA/DPA,PA-2/DPA-3** (38 not indicated in military balance 2018, assumed to be Mirage 5)
Navy (Active personnel) 	58,350 (Reserves 55,000) **Aircraft Carriers** 1 **Submarines** 14 **Destroyers** 14 **Frigates** 13 **Patrol and Coastal** **Combatants** (**Corvettes/Missile Craft**) 108	23,800 (Reserves 5,000) **Aircraft Carriers** None **Submarines** 8 **Destroyers** 0 **Frigates** 10 **Patrol and Coastal** **Combatants** 17 (**Corvettes/Missile Craft**)

> **Source: The IISS Military Balance 2018,**[130]

The Overall Military Imbalance

American intelligence experts privately estimate that the Pakistan Armed Forces could defeat against an Indian invasion for only a few days to a few weeks. This accurately reflects the numerical imbalance in each side's force strength and order of battle. Pakistan will do better on the defensive than in the attack. India has superior static defence capabilities and the mass to counterattack quickly and effectively. Pakistan forces, however, are better structured for a manoeuvre style of warfare and could inflict serious losses on any invading force. And keeping in view the above mentioned Indian superiority in conventional arms, Pakistan then chose to take shelter under the nuclear umbrella.[131]

Pakistan's sees only one major motive for building this large military establishment, which it perceives far beyond its legitimate defence and security requirements can only be found in India's desire for regional hegemony.[132] Indian perceptions of threat to her sovereignty from her small neighbours emerge from its own past and present policies of attempting to subdue the whole of South Asia to her will.

Pakistan Army Personnel along with mechanized troops in the training exercise 'Al Buraq II' held at Kotri Field Firing Ranges.

The strategies employed by both India and Pakistan have all began to evolve over the last few decades. They have changed due to the technological requirements and the adversaries capabilities. We will look at the following strategies in detail, **India's Cold Start doctrine (CSD)** and **Pakistan's New Concept of War Fighting (NCWF):**

---

[130] IISS, Chapter 6 Asia
[131] Cordesman, op cit:131
[132] Malik, op cit:152

India – Cold Start Military doctrine

Cold Start is an evolving doctrine undertaken by the Indian Armed Forces as a counter-measure to the Pakistani Armed Forces under the shadow of two declared nuclear powers. Under the nuclear umbrella, war becomes dangerously a non-option as any misadventure moves could escalate tensions to a nuclear exchange. The potential nuclear exchange would devastate the South Asian region as well effect the global environment.

Indian army chief General Bipin Rawat

The Indian Armed Forces have devised the 'cold start' doctrine as a way initiating a limited rapid conflict and believes that the limited attack on Pakistan would not force Pakistan to use its nuclear weapons. The Indian Armed Forces had denied that any such doctrine existed and it was only when the Indian army chief, Bipin Rawat confirmed its existence in an interview.[133]

Cold Start in essence is a limited war strategy that envisages of seizing Pakistani territory on a rapid basis without resorting to any nuclear exchange. The strategy believes that it can take Pakistani territory before it crosses the Pakistani 'red lines' and hence believe that Pakistan would not resort to a nuclear strike – which could result in a full scale nuclear war. The doctrine has its root from the terrorist attacks on the Indian Parliament in 2001 and was thought to have been masterminded in Pakistan (which has robustly denied any form of involvement). Any terrorist attack in India that is assumed to come from Pakistan would trigger India to put into action its Cold Start doctrine.

The resulting terrorist attack on its parliament and the slow mobilisation of its Strike Corps to the borders with Pakistan resulted in Pakistan rapidly strengthening its defensive positions and thereby nullifying any impending attach from India (by increasing the costs of an incursion and whether it can succeed in its objectives). Cold Start is a strategy to improve this in the future – by essentially having a well organised and special integrated units that are stationed closer to the border would enable India to inflict serious harm before any international pressure to stop hostilities and by pursuing its limited aims, it is assumed that this will deny Pakistan a justification of launching a nuclear strike.

In contrast to the Cold Start doctrine, Pakistan's Prime Minister Shahid Khaqan Abbasi has confirmed that the short range nuclear missile has been developed to counter India's flawed cold start strategy.[134] The Basic evolution of the Cold Start doctrine, is as follows:

1. The terrorist incident on 13 December 2001 was blamed on Pakistan and led to widespread pressures on the Indian Government to take punitive action on its neighbour.

2. Operation Parakram was initiated and Indian troops were mobilised to take action against Pakistan. However, by the time the Indian army's three mechanised strike corps were mobilised to the border and were ready to launch their tanks and infantry combat vehicles (all tools at its disposal), Pakistan's defensive formations were deployed and ready to counter-attack and beat the Indian strike formations with its own strike divisions.[135]

---

[133] https://www.economist.com/blogs/economist-explains/2017/02/economist-explains

[134] http://www.livemint.com/Politics/hpSChKODtfe7Pba34i2rOJ/Cold-Start-doctrine-A-10point-guide-to-Indias-military-st.html

[135] https://thewire.in/101586/cold-start-pakistan-doctrine/

3. It took three weeks for India's Three Strike corps to mobilise and take up positions on the border with Pakistan. This allowed Pakistan to further strengthen its defensive positions and reduced the element of surprise and ensured that the Indian attack would become costly (and could lead to a nuclear strike).

4. Furthermore, this delay in mobilising enabled other international players, such as the US to pressurise India to stop any planned hostilities against Pakistan. The US and its allies had their own interest and were on an offensive against Taliban forces in Afghanistan and did not want Pakistan to stop this as it would affect the logistics of operations in Afghanistan.

5. The slow mobilisation from the Indian Strike Corps led to the development of the Cold Start doctrine. This doctrine plans to attack Pakistan (by rapidly mobilising infantry and armour to launch lightning strikes across the border) within 48 hours of any major provocation or terror attack (that is linked to Pakistan). The plan is to strike and penetrate into Pakistan before its defensive formations can prepare and occupy defensive positions along the border without escalating into a nuclear war.

6. Cold Start is based on two key goals. The first is to readjust its 'Pivot' corps (defensive or ground holding corps) so that it can launch an offensive operation virtually from a 'cold start' and deny Pakistan the advantage of early mobilisation. The second goal was to ensure that India had a number of integrated divisional-size forces launching operations to capture Pakistani territory along the international boundary. The plan is for the integrated battle groups (IBGs) to allow India's strike corps to take advantages of any success achieved. Any captured Pakistani territory would be used as a bargaining tools to stop any alleged proxy war support. These IBGs are to be fully integrated with the Indian Air Force, Naval aviation and to be able to launch multiple strikes round the clock into Pakistan. It is thought that each IBG will be the size of a division (30,000-50,000 troops) and highly mobile unlike the main strike corps.

7. The Indian Military believes that the cold start doctrine would deter Pakistan from waging any proxy war or major provocation by sending a clear message of Indian capability to attack. However, Pakistan sees this as a dangerous doctrine that is inherently escalatory, by forcing the Pakistani armed forces into relocating defensive formations close to the Indian border. In addition, it has compelled the Pakistan army to develop its 'Nasr' (Hatf-IX victory) short-range nuclear missile (small yield nuclear bomb), this is a highly destabilising "tactical nuclear weapons" (TNWs) – to halt an Indian Cold Start strike.

The Indian army has inducted the Russian BM-30 Smerch 300MM multiple-launch rocket systems (MLRS). The Smerch has 300mm rockets with a firing range of 70 - 90 km and able to fire a salvo of 12 rockets in 38 seconds) and could neutralise a large target area.

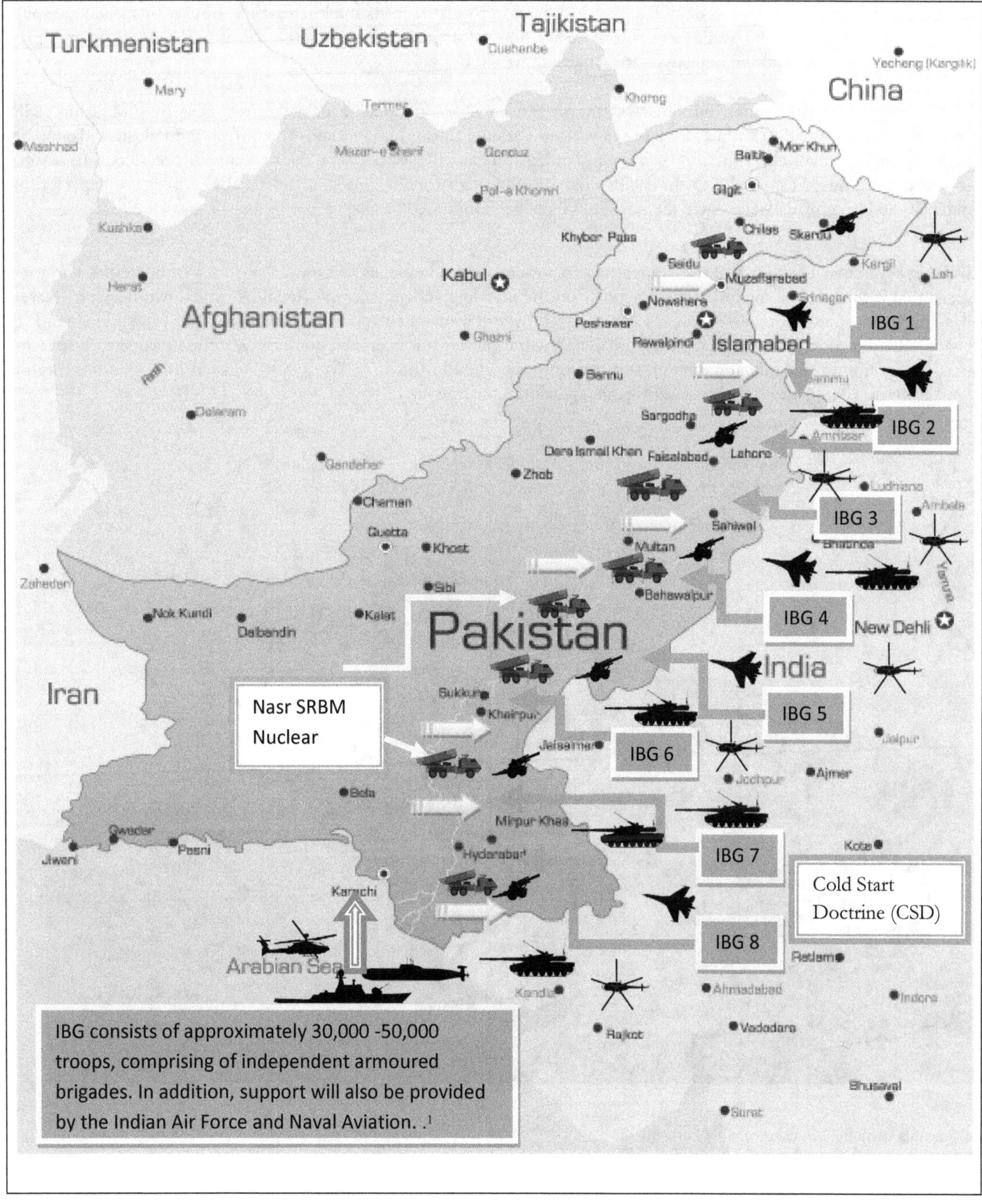

IBG consists of approximately 30,000 -50,000 troops, comprising of independent armoured brigades. In addition, support will also be provided by the Indian Air Force and Naval Aviation. .[1]

> The Cold Start doctrine aims to deny Pakistan justification to resort to its nuclear first-use option by inflicting rapid, fatal and limited attacks.[136] The air force and naval aviation would accompany the land forces in the single or multiples strikes in a limited area till the objectives are achieved "within hours". [137]

Through Cold Start doctrine, India believes that it can paralyse or reduce a Pakistani response by mobilising eight IBGs to enter its territory within 72-96 hours when instructed to do. India intends to confuse the Pakistani troops by breaking their formational cohesion by the rapid attckes of the IBG forces. The confusion will force Pakistan troops to make more mistakes, similar to the 1940s German blitkrieg of its neighbours. India's IBG forces are expected to make 50-80 km teritorial gains once the hostilities have been inititated.

India believes that Pakistan will not launch its short-range nuclear missiles (Nasr) at the outset of hostilities and presume that if they do use tactical nuclear missiles on the invading Indian troops – it will be on its own territory. Naser has an estimated range of 60-70 km. This is agin a folly and a miscalculation on the Indian side – hostilities tend to change the direction of the conflict. India in all its frustration has not been able to decively defeat Pakistan, despite its massive economic and military strength – it had only suceeded in the 1971 War, with Pakistan losing its territory of East Pakistan (Bangladesh) due to a big foreign sponsored insurgency.

Pakistan's battlefield nuclear capable Nasr missile

---

[136] Naveed Ahmed (2017) India's Elusive Cold Start doctrine - https://tribune.com.pk/story/1300686/indias-elusive-cold-start-doctrine-pakistans-military-preparedness/

[137] Masood Ur Rehman Khattak – Indian Military's Cold Start Doctrine RP-32-Masood-Indian-Militarys-Cold-Start-Doctrine-Mar-2011.pdf

Pakistan armed forces have taken a number of measures to deal with India's desire for regional hegemonistic tendencies, where it can brow beat its neighbours. It too has evolved its own strategies to deal with the threat to its territorial integrity and its dispute over Kashmir. India's leaders are continuing their hostile behavious against their neighbour – with the Hindu fundamentalist government of the BJP, Prime minister Narendra Modi has continued with the hostile posturing at a different levels, in the same way as the former BJP prime minister Atal Bihari Vajpayee had done when it conducted its second nuclear test in Pokran. Since Vajpayee tested nuclear weapons in 1998, Pakistan does not believe in India's stance of no-first use. This is more paramount in the current era in which Pakistan is prepared for India opting to nuclear first-use - especially with the current hawkish hindu fundamentalists like Manohar Parrikar, Ajit Davol and Sushma Sawraj at the helm of the BJP government.[138]

For Pakistan, its battle hardened armed forces have adapted to undertake any future hostilities from India or other external threats. The 17 years of conflict in Afghanistan and its spill effect on Pakistan territory via numerous terrorism has enable Pakistan to successfully deal with this threat.

Pakistan has significantly upgraded its defence preparedness and refinement of its military doctrine. It has increased joint operations training amongst all it services. It's refined New Concept of Warfare has been developed to deal with all forms of threats, especially its Cold Start doctrine.

A100 multiple-launch rocket systems (MLRS) of the Pakistani Army

---

[138] https://tribune.com.pk/story/1300686/indias-elusive-cold-start-doctrine-pakistans-military-preparedness

Key Elements in the Indian Cold Start doctrine (CSD)

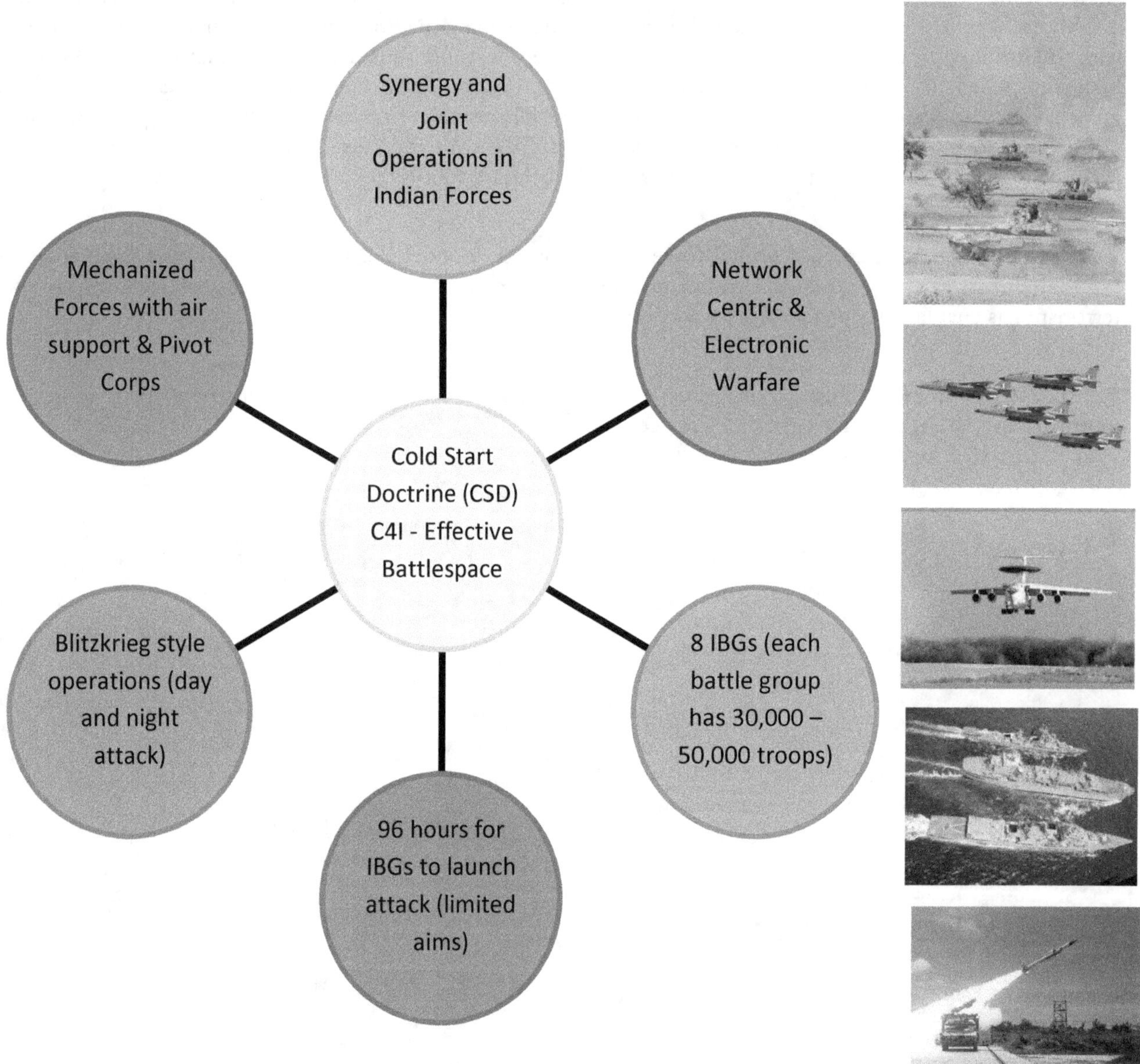

Effective battlespace is term used to signify a unified and integrated military strategy to achieve an overall mission objectives in combined operations. A combination , information, air, land, sea, cyber warfare, space and evolving technologies to achieve military goals. In order to apply effective combat power, other factors such as the environment/terrain, hostile and friendly forces disposition, weather and the area of the influence. In addition, a a robust Command, Control, Communications, Computers, and Intelligence (C4I) needs to be integrated to ensure a decisive edge is maintained of the battlespace."[139]

---

[139] http://www.c4i.org/whatisc4i.html

An Indian air force SU-30K Flanker lands at Gwalior Air Force Station India.[140]

Indian Air Force Su-30MKI fire power demonstration in Pokhran, India.[141]

---

[140] U.S. Air Force photo by Tech. Sgt. Keith Brown http://www.af.mil/shared/media/photodb/photos/040224-F-0000S-007.jpg

[141] Pranab Mukherjee, PM Modi to attend IAF fire power demonstration in Pokhran today - https://www.indiatoday.in/india/story/pranab-modi-to-attend-iafs-fire-power-demonstration-in-pokhran-today-313814-2016-03-18

Formation of IAF Sepecat Jaguar attack/strike aircraft[142]

IAF Jaguar releasing its bombs[143]

---

[142]Indian Air Force - http://indianairforce.nic.in/photo-gallery/40
[143] Indian Air Force - http://indianairforce.nic.in/photo-gallery/8

IAF Su-30 MKI and Jaguar aircraft[144]

Test firing of the Akash missile. A medium-range surface-to-air missile. Operating in conjunction with the Rajendra radar, it can intercept targets up to 30 km range and 18 km altitude. Powered by a solid-fuelled booster and a Ramjet engine, Akash can reach Mach 2.5 speed.[145]

---

[144] Indian Air Force - http://indianairforce.nic.in/#
[145] https://en.wikipedia.org/wiki/Indian_Air_Force#/media/File:Akash_SAM.jpg

Indian Army soldiers with the 99th Mountain Brigade's 2nd Battalion, 5th Gurkha Rifles, execute an ambush for paratroopers with the U.S. Army's 1st Brigade Combat Team, 82nd Airborne Division, May 7, 2013, at Fort Bragg, N.C.[146]

An Indian Air Force chopper (Mi-35 Hind) demonstrates its combat and firepower during 'Exercise Iron Fist' in the desert of Pokhran[147]

---

[146] Sgt. Michael J. MacLeod - http://www.army.mil/media/295122

[147] IRON FIST: IAF showcases mighty firepower at Pokhran - http://www.rediff.com/news/report/iron-fist-iaf-showcases-mighty-firepower-at-pokhran/20160319.htm

MBT[148]

An Arjun MBT being test driven on the bump track at the Central Vehicles Research and Development Establishment (CVRDE), at Avadi, Chennai[149]

Combat Team composed of T72M MBTs, T90S MBTs (possibly) and BMP2 IFVs forming up for an training assault on an enemy held position 02 January 2006[150][151]

[148] https://www.flickr.com/photos/76481380@N00/137395772

[149] Ajai Shukla – ajaishukla.blogspot.com

[150] cell105 - https://www.flickr.com/photos/cell105/110189349/in/album-72057594078654413/

[151] https://www.flickr.com/photos/cell105/3153851416/in/album-72057594078654413/

Indian Navy flotilla of Western Fleet escort INS Vikramaditya (R33) and INS Viraat (R22) in the Arabian Sea[152]

Indian Navy MIG-29K Fulcrum flies over the aircraft carrier USS Nimitz (CVN 68) during Exercise Malabar 2017.[153]

---

[152]

https://en.wikipedia.org/wiki/Indian_Navy#/media/File:Indian_Navy_flotilla_of_Western_Fleet_escort_INS_Vikramaditya_(R_33)_and_INS_Viraat_(R22)_in_the_Arabian_Sea.jpg

[153] U.S. Navy - http://www.navy.mil/management/photodb/photos/170716-N-OV009-063.JPG

INS Chakra, an Indian nuclear submarine leased from Russia.[154]

An Indian Agni-II intermediate range ballistic missile on a road-mobile launcher, displayed at the Republic Day Parade on New Delhi's Rajpath, January 26, 2004.[155]

---

[154] https://en.wikipedia.org/wiki/Indian_Navy#/media/File:INS_Chakra.jpg

Pakistan's New Concept of War Fighting (NCWF):

In order to counter India's Cold Start doctrine (CSD), Pakistan has refined its own strategy and this has now evolved into a New Concept of War Fighting (NCWF) doctrine. This Pakistani doctrine is seen as a major counter balance to India's CSD.[156]

Pakistan military exercises, Azm-e-Nau.

The Azm-e-Nau (New Resolve) Games took place from 2009 -2013 and were essentially exercises to validate Pakistan's new doctrine (NCWF). The war games were the largest ever conducted by the Pakistan armed forces since

---

[155] https://en.wikipedia.org/wiki/India_and_weapons_of_mass_destruction#/media/File:Agni-II_missile_(Republic_Day_Parade_2004).jpeg

[156] Pakistan develops new war doctrine to counter India - https://www.indiatoday.in/world/story/pakistan-develops-new-war-doctrine-to-counter-india-166997-2013-06-17

the Zarb-e-Momin exercises held in 1989 – which had validated its 'offensive defence' doctrine at the time.[157] According to the Inter-Services Public Relations (ISPR), the war games were meant to operationalize new strategies against evolving threats in the country. The conclusion of the 4 years of war gaming and exercises resulted in Pakistani military adopting the new NCWF doctrine, primarily aimed ad pre-empting/disrupting Indians CSD.[158]

The exercises had involved between 30,000- 50,000 troops with the usage of various aircraft and equipment of the Pakistan Air Force. The exercises were conducted whilst 150,000 troops were still engaged in the fight with the Taliban (TTP) on its western border. This new resolve indicated to Pakistan's adversaries that it is able to defend any part of its territory – whether western or eastern border.

The key areas of the NCWF are as follows:

- Improve mobilisation
- Joint coordination of the Army, Air Force and Navy response to any conventional threat.

According to Brigadier Dr Muhammad Khan, Azm-e-Nau puts a checkmate to India's CSD.[159] The war games/exercises were conducted in different phases to test and evaluate different mission scenarios.

Phase-I	In this phase, various scenarios were given and executed and appropriate military plans were refined after evaluation of the exercises (at this stage, it was primarily indoor war games, consisting of substantial map exercises. In addition, numerous operational constraints were injected in to the scenarios and further evaluations were made at the execution of the plans.
Phase-II	The operational plans from phase 1 were executed through physical trials in the field exercises. Any hurdles or shortcomings were further refined after putting the troops through the exercises. The Pakistan Air Force (PAF) and the Pakistan Navy (PN) also participated in these exercises.
Phase-III	Further refinements are made – troops are split in to two groups, Blue Land (defendant) and Fox land (enemy) are put to their paces in the battleground. Mechanised forces (Tanks/armoured personnel carriers), with combination of support provided by the PAF and PN. Conventional firepower of all types has been demonstrated, enhanced training in intelligence gathering, surveillance, reconnaissance and communication means have been checked (network centric warfare capabilities).
Phase IV	The final phase of the war games were undertaken during June 2013. The PAF and the PN have jointly worked with the Army and increased the synergy and integration amongst the services. This was shown by the impressive demonstrations of the armoured, artillery, air defence, army aviation formations and firepower by the PAFs F-16, JF-17 Thunder, F 7P and Mirage fighter aircraft (repelling attacks by enemy forces). The war games were carried out with different formations and at different levels – this was to increase combat readiness, and to identify problems in logistics, training, and to validate its new military doctrine (NCWF).

These exercises had evolved into making the New Concept of War Fighting (NCWF) an updated doctrine for the Pakistan Armed Forces – it is believed to have countered India's Cold start doctrine (CSD) effectively.

---

[157] Azm-e-Nau 3: Largest Military Exercise by Pakistan Army - http://www.chowrangi.pk/azm-e-nau-3-largest-military-exercise-by-pakistan-army.html

[158] Pakistan develops new war doctrine to counter India - https://www.indiatoday.in/world/story/pakistan-develops-new-war-doctrine-to-counter-india-166997-2013-06-17

[159] Brig Dr Muhammad Khan - http://hilal.gov.pk/index.php/component/k2/item/642-from-cold-start-to-cold-storage

Azm-e-Nau (New resolve), demonstration of Pakistani Firepower

Pakistan displays firepower in Arabian Sea

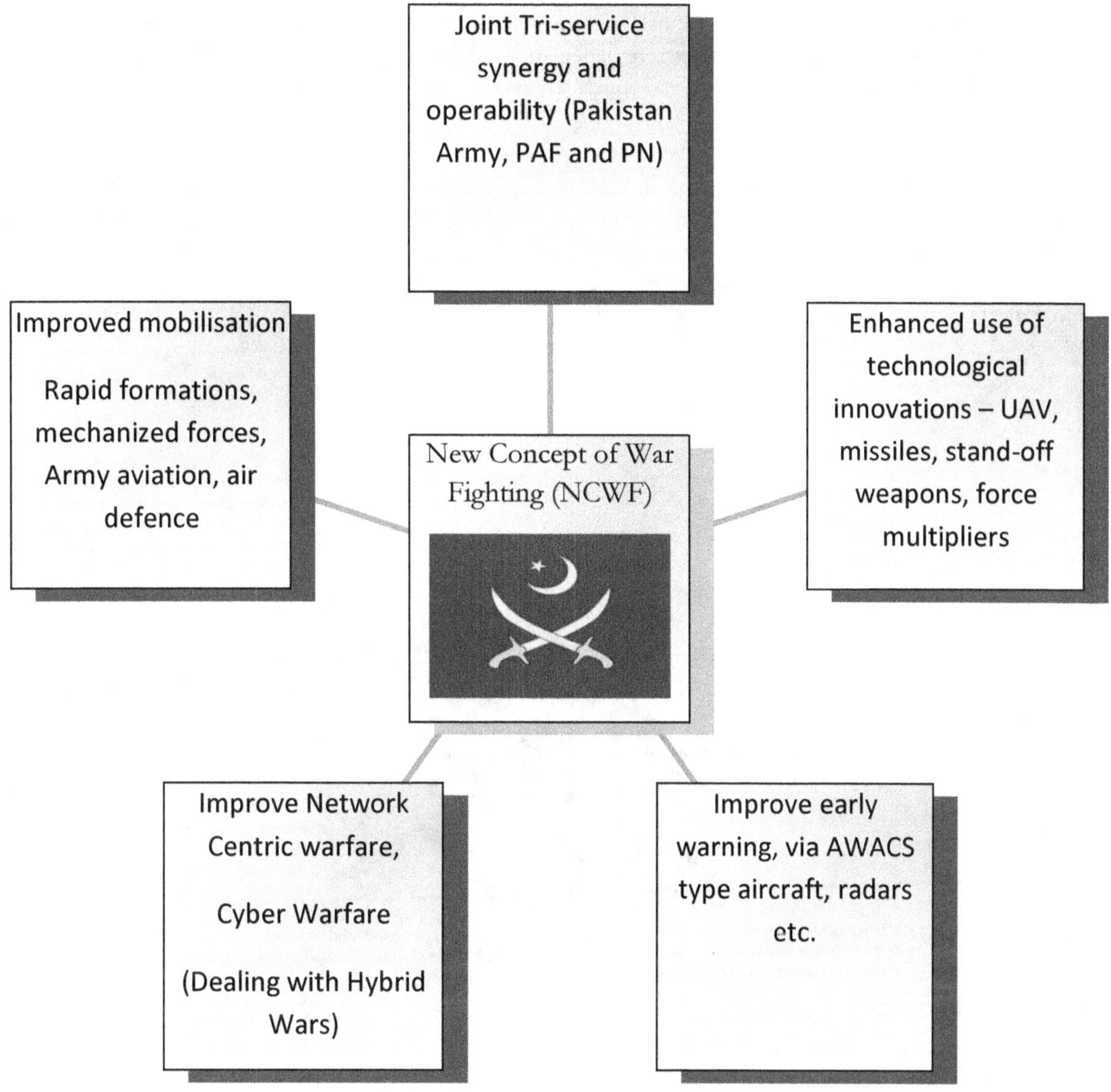

In essence the Pakistan Armed Forces have the capability to detect Indian troop movements due to smaller distances and its increasing force multiplier technologies (AWACS, Reconnaissance etc.) that will give it early warning on enemy forces. For instance:

- Indian troop movements will be detected by Pakistani surveillance assets (AWACS, Radars, UAVs and satellites etc.).
- Rapid mobilisations of Pakistan's holding corps and defensive formations will done within 36–48 hours, this will be faster mobilisation than the Indian CSD can do.
- By the time the Indians actually transgress into Pakistani territory, the Pakistan Armed Forces will be well prepared to defend as they would have received significant time to bolster their defences and offensive capabilities.

- Due to a high level of synergy and interoperability between the Pakistan Army, PAF and the PN, tri-service air support for the troops fighting in the ground will be readily available.
- Force multiplier capabilities and advance technologies, would enhance Pakistan's defensive and offensive capabilities – increased situational awareness via network centric technologies, evolving UCAV/UAV capabilities ranging from surveillance and intelligence gathering to artillery fire correction, target acquisition and AGM capability would blunt an Indian attack and enable offensive manoeuvres into Indian territory.

Hence, Pakistan's New Concept of War Fighting (NCWF) is able to address the country's conventional capabilities as well as its nuclear. [160] Since Exercise 'Zarb-i-Momin' was conducted in 1989, there has been a radical change in Indian war fighting doctrine (Cold Start Doctrine) which Pakistan has been trying to counter from a conventional and nuclear aspect. Exercise Azm-e-Nau (New Resolve) had evolved into making the New Concept of War Fighting (NCWF) an updated doctrine for the Pakistan Armed Forces.

Mi-35 Hind Gunship helicopter[161]

---

[160] Pakistan claims to have developed NCWF to counter India's Cold Start Doctrine - http://defencenews.in/article/Pakistan-claims-to-have-developed-NCWF-to-counter-Indias-Cold-Start-Doctrine---Pak-Media-251068

[161] https://pixabay.com/en/helicopter-free-military-helicopter-2198359/

View of Army field exercise Azm-e- Nau 4 being held near Khairan (02-11-2013)[162]

Azm-e-Nau 4 Heavy mechanised forces [163]

[162] https://www.ispr.gov.pk/front/t-press_release.asp?id=2408&print=1

[163] https://www.ispr.gov.pk/front/image_viewer.asp?o=5630.jpg

Azm-e-Nau 4 PAF F-16 Falcons[164]

Azm-e-Nau 4 Air Defence guns[165]

---

[164] https://www.ispr.gov.pk/front/image_viewer.asp?o=5618.jpg

[165] https://www.ispr.gov.pk/front/image_viewer.asp?o=5634.jpg

Azm-e-Nau 4 troops training in all conditions, including night operations[166]

Azm-e-Nau 4 APC on a training at night[167]

---

[166] https://www.pakistanarmy.gov.pk/AWPReview/ImageEnlarged.aspx?GalleryID=148&ImageID=2251
[167] https://www.pakistanarmy.gov.pk/AWPReview/ImageEnlarged.aspx?GalleryID=148&ImageID=2284

Azm-e-Nau 4 Main battle tank on exercise[168]

Azm-e-Nau 3 T-80UD MBT[169]

---

[168] https://www.pakistanarmy.gov.pk/AWPReview/ImageEnlarged.aspx?GalleryID=148&ImageID=2283

[169] https://www.pakistanarmy.gov.pk/AWPReview/ImageEnlarged.aspx?GalleryID=95&ImageID=1090

Pakistani soldier with the MG-3 Machine gun on a security patrol

Pakistan Army soldier on a security operation

June 17, 2014 Pakistan army in for long haul in offensive against TTP/Taliban[170]

Pakistani troops in action[171]

---

[170] https://www.dawn.com/news/1113336/pakistan-army-in-for-long-haul-in-offensive-against-taliban

[171] https://tribune.com.pk/story/716558/economic-survey-13-year-war-on-terror-cost-102-5-billion/

Air to air refueling with PAF Mirages– JF-17 has also the capability to do this and will gradually take over this role [172]

---

[172] http://www.paf.gov.pk/wallpapers/IL_78_1.jpg

PAF Mirage combat aircraft

PAF F-16B MLU from No.11 Sqn dropping a pair of 2000lbs each

Pakistan Navy establishes Task Force 88 to safeguard CPEC, Gwadar port[173]

Pakistani Navy ships on patrol in the Arabian Sea

<hr>

[173] Pak Navy establishes Task Force 88 to safeguard CPEC, Gwadar port - https://www.thenews.com.pk/latest/171584-Pak-Navy-establishes-Task-Force-88-to-safeguard-CPEC-Gwadar-port

SSG commandos of Pakistan Navy are the only special forces of Pakistan who are capable of doing operations at sea-level, under-water, land and space.[174]

SSG commandos of Pakistan Navy

---

[174] PN SSG Commandos – https://www.thenews.com.pk/latest/195273-Golden-Jubilee-of-Pak-Navy-Special-Services-Group-being-celebrated-today

PNS Aslat on a training exercise[175]

PN sailors and PNS Ship firing the 'Harba' anti-ship/land attack missile

---

[175] Pakistan Navy Frigate PNS Aslat Conducts Counter Drug Operation in Arabian Sea –
https://defpost.com/pakistan-navy-frigate-pns-aslat-conducts-counter-drug-operation-arabian-sea/

Pakistan Navy personnel and PNS Submarine on a training mission

Pakistan Navy's Z-9C Anti-submarine warfare (ASW) Helicopter

PN tests of the nuclear capable Babur 3 SLCM which will add to the deterrence in the region

Pakistan Soldiers on a counterinsurgency operation

Pakistani SSG on a training ecercise with chinese special forces

Chapter 6: The Nuclear Option and Regional Deterrence

Pakistani military personnel stand beside long-range ballistic Shaheen I missiles during the Pakistan Day military parade in Islamabad

Since the end of the Cold War period, nuclear weapons have been reduced from a massive 70,300 warheads in 1986 to an estimated 14,550 bombs in 2017.[176] In 2017 the following nine countries possessed nuclear weapons and all have been developing a number of methods to launch nuclear weapons to deter any would be adversary (land-based intercontinental ballistic missiles, strategic bombers, and submarine-launched ballistic missiles) - the USA, Russia, UK, France, China, India, Pakistan, Israel and North Korea possess nuclear weapons.[177]

All the nuclear powers have either developed or are in the process of developing different technologies to ensure that they are able to deter a would be adversary. New ballistic missiles, air launched cruise missiles (ALCM), ground (GLCM) and sea based nuclear delivery systems are being pursued by the nuclear powers.[178]

---

[176] https://fas.org/issues/nuclear-weapons/status-world-nuclear-forces/

[177] https://www.sipri.org/media/press-release/2017/global-nuclear-weapons-modernization-remains-priority

[178] https://www.armscontrol.org/factsheets/Nuclearweaponswhohaswhat

Table 1. World nuclear forces, 2017

Country	Year of first nuclear test	Deployed warheads*	Other warheads	Total 2017
USA	1945	1,800	5,000	6,800
Russia	1949	1,950	5,050	7,000
UK	1952	120	95	215
France	1960	280	20	300
China	1964		270	270
India	1974		120–130	120–130
Pakistan	1998		130–140	130–140
Israel	. .		80	80
North Korea	2006		10-20	10-20
Total		**4,150**	**10,785**	**14,935**

* Deployed warheads refers to warheads placed on missiles or located on bases with operational forces. ** Other warheads refers to warheads that are held in reserve or that are retired and awaiting dismantlement. SIPRI Yearbook 2017.

https://www.sipri.org/media/press-release/2017/global-nuclear-weapons-modernization-remains-priority

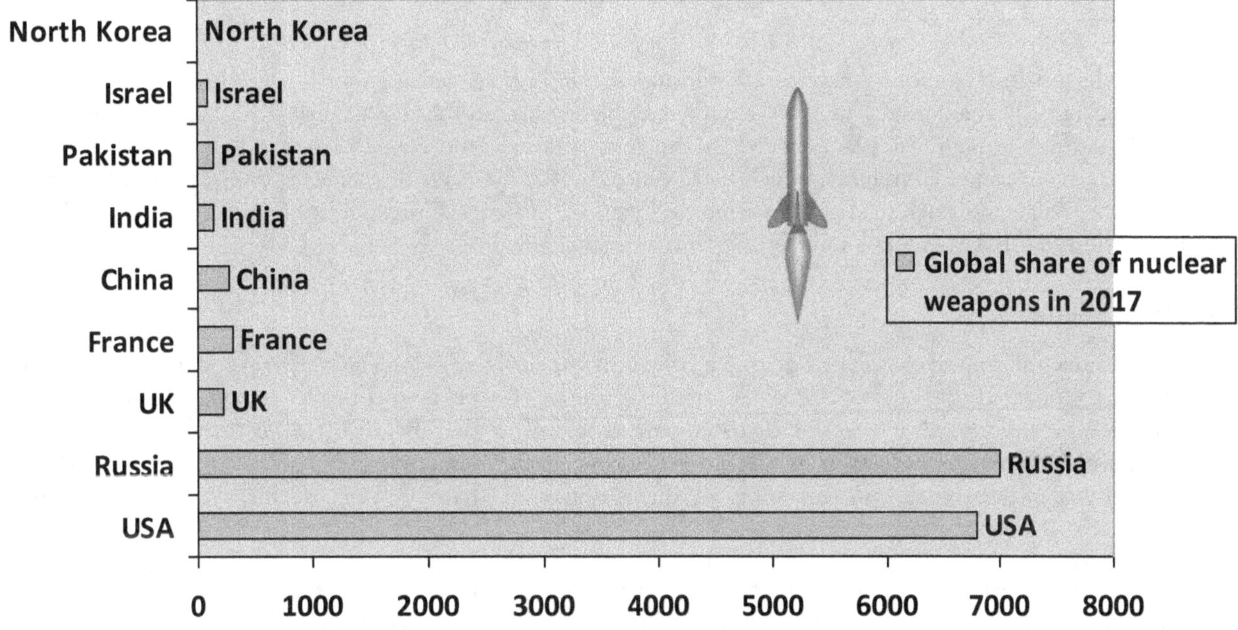

USA	Russia	UK	France	China	India	Pakistan	North Korea	Israel
6,800	7,000	215	300	270	130	140	20	80

https://fas.org/issues/nuclear-weapons/status-world-nuclear-forces/

The Nuclear Option and Regional Deterrence

The principle reason for nuclear and missile proliferation in the Indian sub-continent is the rivalry between India and Pakistan. The security dynamics of the region are complicated further by India's threat perception of China. Pakistan's efforts to develop nuclear delivery systems are intended primarily to counter India's substantial conventional military advantage and its perception of India's nuclear threat.[179]

India started on the road to nuclear autonomy after 1962s border clashes between India and China,[180] which was followed by China going nuclear in 1964.[181] Despite improved relations recently, China is perceived as a long-term threat by India. Secondary to this threat perception is India's ambition to achieve regional hegemony and global prestige. It has long aspired for a permanent seat on the UN Security Council and India's policymakers believed that this was only possible if India was a declared nuclear power.[182]

Pakistan began its nuclear weapons program after losing the 1971 war, accelerating it in response to India's 1974 nuclear test. Pakistan's Prime Minister in 1974, Zulifikar Bhutto, declared that Pakistanis would 'eat grass' rather than surrender the nuclear option.[183] Bhutto believed the nuclear option would give Pakistan a military countermeasure against India's large conventional military, which had been strengthened even further with the possibility of a nuclear device. Like India, Pakistan's nuclear status has become a symbol of national prestige, adding to the average Pakistani citizen's perception that Pakistan was a military match for India at any time.[184]

India Shocks the World

On May 1998, India announced that it had detonated five nuclear devices,[185] under the pretext of a potential security threat. This led to Pakistan testing its own devices within a matter of weeks, in order to 'balance the security of the region'.[186] India also announced a weapons development program, to the chagrin of international opinion. Critics argue that India's decision was devoid of a strategic rationale- it went against India's own 50-year old principles of opposition to nuclear deterrence, and rejection of the proposition that weapons of mass destruction generate security.[187]

Upon inspection, India has failed to justify its reasons for accelerating nuclear proliferation in the region. There has been no deterioration in India's security environment in recent years. On the contrary, India has improved relations with its neighbours, especially China. The Indian drive toward nuclear weapons capability had also not been fuelled by any necessity to check Pakistan. India, with its superior conventional strength, did not need nuclear weapons to counter a then non-nuclear Pakistan. Nor had India been under serious pressure to sign unequal arms control agreements. It seems obvious that the BJP was clearing the ground for India's hegemonic agenda.[188]

Several observers of the South Asian scene have argued that neither China nor Pakistan have posed any increased

---

[179] Fareed Zakaria, How to be a Great Cheap, NewsWeek, T.P.L Printers Ltd, May 25, 1998, Pg26

[180] Ibid

[181] Paul Rogers, Guide to Nuclear Weapons 1984-85, C.J.W Printers Ltd, 1984, Pg88

[182] Zakaria op cit:26

[183] Nils Bhinda, The Kashmir Conflict-1990, Earthscan Publication Ltd, 1994, Pg72

[184] Ibid

[185] India Today, India is now a nuclear weapons state, Living India Media Ltd, May 1998, Pg12

[186] India Today, Pakistan's nuclear test, what now, June 1998, Pg14

[187] Ibid

[188] Eric Arnett, What Threat?, Bulletin of the Atomic Scientists, 1997, Pg53

threat to India, leaving little reason for it to go nuclear. The consensus of opinion is that the Hindu fundamentalist government of Prime Minister Vajpayee was desperate to consolidate the power it had strived for since India's independence. Indeed, their election manifesto had been built around the premise of reviving India's nuclear program.

According to Lawrence Freedman, Professor of War Studies (Kings College), the real reasons for testing its nuclear device was,

"The answer lies in the election of a hawkish Indian government. It has offered the strategic rationale that nuclear weapons are still needed to deter a Chinese threat – despite the apparent relaxation of relations between these two giant countries in recent years – and the need to keep Pakistan in check. More important, however, are questions of national pride. The Indian nuclear debate has always proceeded on the assumption that nuclear status really matters when it comes to setting the international hierarchy".[189]

On Pakistan's reasons for conducting its nuclear device, Freedman said, **"Once India has detonated its weapons, Pakistan really had little choice. It is smaller than India and much weaker, both economically and militarily. It had to prove its own nuclear capacity to reassure its population that India could be deterred".[190]**

He also said, **"Given that neither China nor the U.S could offer Pakistan a nuclear guarantee as an alternative, its options were limited".[191]**

India's BJP government is known for anti-Muslim stance. BJP was responsible for the destruction of the famous 16th century Babri mosque.[192] BJP, before coming to power, vowed to retake Azaad (free) Kashmir from Pakistan.[193] Home Minister L K Advani made a statement that the strategic scenario in the subcontinent has changed dramatically after the current round of Indian tests. He also did not rule out limited military strikes across the border at insurgency training camps in Pakistan. After the Indian tests, India's Home Minister L K Advani spelt out the Indian intent, He said

"Islamabad should realise the change in the geo-strategic situation in the region and the world and rollback its anti-India policy, especially with regard to Kashmir".[194]

And that **"India's bold and decisive step to become a nuclear-weapon state has brought about a qualitatively new stage in Indo-Pakistan relations, particularly in finding a solution to the Kashmir problem".[195]**

And that it **"signifies India's resolve to deal firmly and strongly with Pakistan's hostile designs and activities in Kashmir",** and that India will now take **'proactive'** measures against Kashmir militancy. Almost as if building a case for a rapid strike Advani referred to the Kashmir separatists as **"foreign mercenaries".[196]**

In the wake of the Indian tests, the weak and indecisive world reaction to the Pokhran explosions convinced Pakistan of the new threats to its security. The first G-8 gathering did not display a tough will to punish India's unprovoked nuclear delinquency. Russia was all but silent. The non-aligned nations meeting in Colombia did not strongly condemn the Indian tests. Above all, the United States was not prepared to offer Pakistan a security guarantee sufficient to allay its heightened fears. In fact, since 1990 the US has refused to deliver 28 F-16s which Pakistan had bought from America and for which it had already paid $658 million years ago.[197]

This had not only weakened Pakistan's conventional defence capability but had also weakened the countries confidence in Washington as a dependable ally. In the light of these circumstances and after India had carried out its nuclear tests, followed by hostile and proactive statements made against Pakistan by Indian leaders (such as L.K

---

[189] Lawrence Freedman, National Pride sets the Sabre Rattling, Daily Mail, May 29, 1998, Pg6

[190] Ibid

[191] Ibid

[192] Edward W. Desmond, Unity or Chaos?, Time November 12, 1990, Pg42

[193] News International, India will have to reclaim Azaad Kashmir says Defence Minister, Jang Publications, Ltd, 1998, Pg1

[194] News International, Advani's Nuclear Blackmail, August 10, 1998, Pg1

[195] Ibid

[196] Ibid

[197] News International, Advani's Nuclear Blackmail, August 10, 1998, Pg1

Advani). And considering the likelihood of an Indian attack on Pakistani-held Kashmir, Pakistani forces were reportedly placed on highest alert. Pakistan then chose to respond in kind, by exploding its own nuclear device at Chagai in its Balochistan province on May 28 and 30.[198]

Once the nuclear capability had been demonstrated, Pakistan achieved strategic parity with India. Indeed, as Indian critics of the BJP's decision pointed out, the Indian test conferred several benefits upon Pakistan: it enabled Pakistan to conduct nuclear tests openly, virtually eliminated India's military edge in conventional weapons, and brought the Kashmir dispute, which was the main cause of Indo-Pakistan tensions, in the global spotlight.[199]

The rise of Hindu fundamentalism

In fact, domestic considerations, not external threats or dissatisfaction with the way the nuclear weapon states have acted, are paramount. One cannot comprehend why India crossed the nuclear threshold without giving decisive weight to the changing self-perceptions of the Indian elite and the profound transformations the country has undergone in the last 10 years with the rise of a viciously sectarian, and deeply belligerent political force, the Bharatiya Janata Party (BJP) and its affiliates.[200]

The BJP, a right-wing reactionary political party established in 1980, propounds an ideology of aggressive anti-Muslim, anti-secular Hindu nationalism. It has made dramatic gains in the past decade: In 1984 the BJP had only two seats in the 543- member Lower House of Parliament; today it is the single largest party with 180 seats, and it heads a coalition government.[201]

Behind the BJP and inseparable from it-is the Rashtriya Swayamsevak Sangh (National Volunteer Corps), which is the real head of an overall combine, called the Bajrang Dal, a huge anti-Muslim cultural force that operates the Vishwa Hindu Parishad (World Hindu Council). The Rashtriya Swayamsevak Sangh (RSS) has fascist characteristics. The RSS does not contest parliamentary elections nor does it hold elections to various organizational posts. It is a secret, all-male organization whose objective is to establish a Hindu state.[202]

The rise of Hindu nationalism has completely altered the discourse of Indian politics and it is beginning to transform the character of Indian society. Nothing else so fully explains why India took the decision to shed its nuclear ambiguity. India's nuclearization reflects the belief of the BJP-RSS as well as growing sections of the Indian elite that nuclear weapons constitute a shortcut to establishing the country's stature as a major actor-in Prime Minister Atal Bihari Vajpayee's words, the nuclear tests "show our strength and silence our enemies".[203]

From the BJP, nuclear weapons are an article of faith, part of the essential identity of a powerful awe-inspiring, militarist Hindu India that can boast of its manliness and virility and thus prove to the world the superiority of Hindu 'civilization'. [204]

Nuclear Deterrence

India-China relations, which had greatly improved in the 1990s with the signing of two major peace agreements in 1991 and 1996, have received a decisive setback, because of India's testing of its nuclear device and the hostile remarks made by Indian ministers. China will now see India as a nuclear rival and act accordingly. India has already declared that its missile development program is meant to create a deterrent against China. India suspects China of being the country most likely to challenge its efforts to emerge as a regional power.[205]

Pakistani leaders believe that a nuclear capability is essential to deter war with India, or failing that, to ensure the survival of the nation. Its nuclear program has widespread political and popular support. Missile procurement and

---

[198] India Today, Bang for Bang, June 1998, Pg10
[199] Zakaria op cit:26
[200] Hewitt, op cit:182
[201] Ibid
[202] Ibid
[203] Sunday Telegraph, India celebrates its Nuclear dream, May 1998, Pg27
[204] Ibid
[205] Arnett op cit:153

development, initially to counter the Indian missile program which began in the mid-1980s, are driven by a desire to augment limited offensive air capabilities against India (which holds almost 2:1 advantage in combat aircraft) and to field a more effective delivery system.[206]

Most Pakistani strategies and military leaders regard the nuclear choice as a prudent strategic bargain. As Pakistan's former Army Chief of Staff, General Mirza Aslam Beg, noted a nuclear deterrent for Pakistan represents "the cheapest option for peace",[207] balancing Indians and Pakistanis see nuclear weapons as an instrument of independence from the United States and other outside powers.

Neither India nor Pakistan regards the current international non-proliferation regime (the NPT) as relevant or helpful to its security problems. India has always regarded the NPT as the centrepiece of a conscious U.S. policy of denying lesser nations access in the fruits of economic and industrial development, to which the world's largest democracy should be entitled. Pakistan has offered to sign the NPT if India does it as well.[208]

However, both sides should take a deep breath and consider the historical lesson of 1962, when the United States and the Soviet Union moved to the brink of nuclear war over Cuba. We now know something we did not know then. Had President Kennedy ordered the invasion of Cuba, Russian commanders in Cuba were under orders from Premier Khruschev to launch nuclear missiles against the United States.[209]

Kashmir in today's Cuba. India and Pakistan are poised to fight over Kashmir, only now they have nuclear weapons to back up their passionate claims to this disputed territory. A miscalculation by either side could result in the unthinkable calamity that the United States and Russia barely avoided in 1962. The consequences of a nuclear war between India and Pakistan would be catastrophic.[210]

Nuclear stockpiles

India has conducted only one nuclear test (1974) until recently, and has conducted five nuclear tests in May 1998. Since the 1974 test, India is believed to have produced some 130 nuclear devices and made significant progress in refining its bomb-making technology.[211] Pakistan has sufficient materials to arm a 140 nuclear weapons.[212]

Nuclear command-and-control

Both India and Pakistan have civilian governments led by a prime-minister. The process of consultation used to arrive at a decision to test nuclear weapons was obviously highly motivated by a small circle in the ruling parties, with the decision taken quickly without public discussions. The decision to use nuclear weapons would undoubtedly be a far more searching and deliberate one.[213] The former Indian Defence Minister George Fernandes told Jane's Defence Weekly that the country is working toward a nuclear command and control system under the exclusive control of a national security council, which is being formed.[214] In Pakistan, where the military has played a larger role in governing the nation (and in initiating and supporting the bomb program) the decision is likely to be even more firmly lodged within an exclusive uniformed circle. The Defence Committee of the Pakistan Cabinet, chaired by the prime-minister, is believed to have taken the final deliberations to test the nuclear devices to respond to India.[215]

Nuclear Doctrine

To go to the effort to build and deploy any arsenal of weapons inexorably brings forth some sort of plan to use them. The more weapons a nation has, and the more types, the more involved and complex the planning becomes. In

---

[206] News International, Armed to the Teeth, 1998, Pg27

[207] Ibid

[208] Ibid

[209] J.A.S Greenville, History of the World, HarperCollins Publishers, 1994, Pg593

[210] Ibid

[211] JDW, Trials provide Data for ranges of weapon Yields, May 1998, Pg3

[212] JDW, Pakistan Needs up to 70 Nuclear Warheads, June 1998, Pg3

[213] JDW, India and Pakistan move to prevent nuclear disaster, March 1999, Pg16

[214] Ibid

[215] Ibid

creating a war plan one starts with a target list. As nuclear war plans evolved in the United States and the Soviet Union there were two basic kinds of targets, "countervalue" and "counterforce".[216]

In the 1950s and 1960s the accuracy of the weapons-whether dropped by plane or delivered by missile was not very good, and thus cities became the "countervalue" targets of choice. As the weapons became more accurate and sophisticated, military, or "counterforce" targets took precedence. The goal of counterforce targeting is to destroy enemy nuclear forces before they can be fired (and destroy yours).[217]

However, targeting and deployments do not take place in a vacuum, and in the history of the Cold War, the ability to target enemy missiles precipitated its own crises and countermeasures. The temptation at least in the "theory" of deterrence to launch first was heightened. "Use-'em-or-lose-'em" was the popular description of this predicament. This might describe Pakistan's doctrine, given its military inferiority to India. After the nuclear tests, Pakistani Prime Minister Nawaz Sharif stated that "Pakistani nuclear weapons will deter aggression, whether nuclear or conventional", suggesting a first-use stance.[218]

Indeed, Pakistan's strategy is similar to the North Atlantic Treaty Organisations (NATO) stance in Europe during the Cold War. NATO realised that it could never match the Warsaw's Pact's conventional might. Therefore, it settled for doctrine that gave it the flexibility to use nuclear weapons first. Pakistan has adopted a similar strategy and hinted that it could contemplate a nuclear first strike if its security were seriously threatened.[219]

Indian and Pakistani targets.

Nuclear targets may be broken down into three major categories: military targets; infrastructure, economic and industrial targets and cities. Military targets include military bases and headquarters, airfields, naval bases and specific nuclear weapons, concentrations of missiles or aircraft, both storage sites and operational units. Infrastructure and economic targets include energy facilities, nuclear reactors, dams, bridges, railroad hubs, factories and the like.[220]

Many military targets are close to major urban concentrations of which South Asia has no shortage. Bombay, Calcutta and Delhi have population of 12, 11 and 8 million respectively. Karachi, Lahore and Rawalpindi have population of 8, 5 and 2 million respectively. One bomb dropped on a large Indian or Pakistani city could cause millions of causalities.[221]

Delivery Vehicles

There has been further analysis and speculation about the nuclear capabilities and equipment of the two nations, including the development of a "triad" of nuclear capabilities by India. Only India has been explicit in its plans to develop a "strategic nuclear force". Pakistan has not stated whether it is set on deploying a dedicated nuclear arsenal, but undoubtedly India's actions will spur Pakistan along to reach India's technological level.[222]

The most likely method that India or Pakistan could use to reliably deliver a nuclear weapon today is by aircraft. Aircrafts were the initial method used by the first five nuclear nations. All initially carried gravity bombs. Later these planes were supplemented and/or replaced by many other types and also by various kinds of air-delivered cruise missiles and land- and –sea- based ballistic missiles.[223]

Nuclear-Capable Aircraft. India and Pakistan have several types of aircraft that would be capable of delivering nuclear weapons. India has a substantial number of fixed-wing aircraft that could be modified to deliver nuclear weapons. These include the Anglo-French Jaguar, the Mirage 2000 and the Soviet-supplied MIG-27 and MIG-29 and the very

---

[216] C.Philips, The Nuclear Casebook, Polygon Books, 1983, Pg16-17
[217] Ibid
[218] News International, Nuclear arms not to be used: Nawaz, June 1998, Pg1
[219] Ibid
[220] Sanat Biswas, Doomsday project, June 1994, Pg 84
[221] Ibid
[222] India Today, Future Fire, May 25, 1998, Pg23
[223] Albright & Zamora, op cit:26

sophisticated state-of-the-art Su-30MKI ultra long range strike aircraft (equivalent to the American F-15E).[224]

According to some sources, the Indian Defence Research and Development Organisation has perfected nuclear bombing techniques using the MIG-23 and MIG-27. For example, in the early 1980s, the Indian Air Force conducted fusing tests to verify that a nuclear bomb could be attached to and successfully released from its aircraft.[225] In 1997 Eric Arnett argued that India's acquisition of 315 Paveway II guidance kits to be used on 2000 Ib bombs as well as unknown number of similar smart weapons from Russia could with the help of its Air Force degrade the Pakistani nuclear strike potential compelling that nation into the "use of or lose it" (First Strike) dilemma and go in for an early or first use of its nuclear potential.[226]

Pakistan's military aircraft include nuclear-capable, U.S. supplied F-16 fighters, French-supplied Mirage 3/5 fighter-bombers and the co-developed Pakistani/Chinese JF-17 Thunder multi-role combat aircrafts. In the 1990 crisis with India over the uprising in Kashmir, Pakistani F-16s were reported to have been armed with nuclear bombs.[227]

<u>Indian and Pakistani missiles.</u> A ballistic missile has advantages and disadvantages: It is more likely to reach its intended target in the face of defensive measures. Each country has strategic reasons for pursuing this option: For India, a missile may be the only 'deterrent' possible against China; for Pakistan, which has a far smaller and less diverse air force than India, missiles may be the only reliable deterrent.[228]

India and Pakistan are developing and may deploy one or more types of ballistic missiles for nuclear weapon delivery. Since the tests, there has also been much speculation about India's sea-based missile capabilities.

<u>Nuclear Submarines.</u> India has been working since 1985 to develop an indigenously constructed nuclear-powered submarine, one that is based on the Soviet Charlie II-class design, detailed drawings of which are said to have been obtained from the Soviet Union in 1989.[229] Once the vessel is completed, around 2001-2005, it will be equipped with Sagarika cruise missiles and an advanced sonar system. The Sagarika began development in 1994 as a submarine-launched cruise missile (SLCM) which will have a range of at least 300 kms; it is projected for deployment around 2005.[230] By 2018, India has now developed and is in the process of testing much longer K-4 series SLBM and Agni series ICBMs.

North Korean Ballistic missile test[231] on March 7, 2017 shows the launch of four ballistic missiles by the Korean People's Army (KPA). This also shows have difficult it would be for a defending nation with a BMD capability to successfully shoot them all down. This is te kind of false narrative and a belief that a BMD capable nation holds resulting in an catastropic destruction of the countries involved.

---

[224] Ibid

[225] Sanat Biswas, Testing Time, 'Sunday Magazine', June 1998, Pg6

[226] Arnett, Nuclear stability and arms sales to India, Arms Control Today, 1997, Pg3

[227] India Today, India and Pakistan hours away from a nuclear war, 1994, Pg22

[228] Jane Nolan, Ballistic Missiles in the Third World, Brookings Institutions, 1991, Pg89

[229] JDW, Nuclear Submarine is being built in India, December 1994, Pg3

[230] Ibid

[231] An Atomic-Weapons Expert's Worst-Case Scenario for What Trump Might Do With All That 'Access to the Nuclear Codes' - http://nymag.com/daily/intelligencer/2017/03/an-atomic-weapons-expert-on-the-worst-case-nuclear-scenario.html

Chapter 7: An emerging Ballistic Missile Race

An Emerging Ballistic Missile Race

One of the most dangerous missile competitions in the world today is the one between India and Pakistan, because they both have nuclear weapons and both have ballistic missiles to deliver them. These missiles could carry either conventional or nuclear weapons. Ballistic missiles are the weapon of choice for many developing nations. Their speed-to-target capabilities, invulnerability to defences, mobility, increasing accuracy and adaptability for carrying nuclear warheads all contribute to their inherently destabilising nature in regional rivalries. The relatively short distances between borders allow even tactical-range systems to have a significant impact upon regional balances.[232] The long-standing feud between the two countries has almost led to a nuclear face-off on at least occasion, in 1990.[233] We will look at the Indian missile threat that Pakistan faces and in the development of its own missile capability.

Indian Missile Forces

India has one of the world's most formidable missile programmes. India's military ballistic missile capabilities have become a lot more sophisticated in recent years. This has almost certainly become possible through India's space programme, which is one of the most advanced among the emerging missile powers.[234]

India started its ballistic missile development programme much earlier than Pakistan, aided in the development and deployment of missiles by both France and Russia. It has demonstrated the capability to launch satellites into orbit and has been a *de-facto* nuclear state since 1974. It has been almost universally accepted that India is well on the way to

---

[232] Nolan op cit:88

[233] Ibid

[234] JDW, Asia's Missile Race Hots up, February 1994, Pg20

developing an intercontinental ballistic missiles (ICBM) with a range of greater than 12,000km.[235]

India's missile programmes are overseen by the Defence Research and Development Organisation (DRDO), which is in turn responsible for India's Integrated Guided Missile Development Programme (IGMDP). In 1983 the IGMDP programme saw the development and flight testing of five missile systems-the surface-to-surface (SSM) Prithvi and Agni missiles, surface-to-air (SAM) Akash and Trishul missiles and the anti-tank missile Nag. Using the experience gained from India's space programme, the IGMDP tested the Prithvi short-range missile in 1988. Though these designs are of concern for all countries in the region, for Pakistan the Prithvi and Agni missile programs have been followed with a greater degree of alarm. Of specific concern is the Prithvi missile, which has been labelled as 'Pakistan specific' by several Pakistani leaders. It is an SRBM with a range of 350km and a CEP (circular error probability) of 250m. It is capable of delivering a nuclear or conventional warhead of up to 1000kg.[236]

There are three variants of this missile: the SS-150, which is a battlefield support version for the Indian Army with a range of 150km and the ability to carry a payload of 1,000kg; the SS-250, which is a short-range missile (250km) with a warhead weight of 500-750 Kg for the Indian Air Force, (user trials are due to begin shortly); and the SS-350, which has a range of 350km and a warhead weight of 750-1,000 kg. Particularly alarming are reports that all versions of the Prithvi are nuclear-capable.[237]

In April, 1997, a minor crisis was sparked when news of Prithvi's deployment on the Pakistani border was leaked in the US press. India had moved its medium range missiles to prospective launch site at the Indo-Pakistan border near Jalandhar.[238] Meanwhile, repeated Indian announcements of induction of missiles (75 Prithvis being ordered by Indian Army and 25 by its airforce),[239] together with identification of missile sites, added up to a pattern of creeping deployment of the Prithvi. By 1996 an unspecified number of Prithvi missiles were believed to be in the possession of the Indian army's elite 333-missile group. This missile allows India to target Pakistan's capital city Islamabad and most of the close proximity defence establishments.[240]

Pakistan's reaction time to the pre-emptive launch of the missile is less than three minutes. Carried on mobile launchers and requiring little preparation time, the mobilisation of the Prithvi missile has marked a significant change in the strategic landscape.[241]

India has also tested its long-range, indigenously developed Agni missile. It is capable of carrying a nuclear payload, and has the potential to hit targets over 1500 kilometres away. The Indian government has also approved and advanced Agni system with a target range of 2500 kilometres, and is currently developing an ICBM called Surya with a range of over 12,000 kilometres.[242]

On the day of its nuclear tests, India test fired a home-made short range missile, the Trishul missile, at Chandipur. The Trishul, with a 50km range, has been developed for the Indian Navy. Russia is also assisting India in developing Sagarika, a 700km range sea-based cruise missile, also capable of a nuclear payload.[243]

Pakistan Missile Forces

Pakistan has escalated its own missile programme after the testing of Agni. However, unlike both Israel and India, Pakistan had no space launch programme at the time and therefore lacked the expertise to develop ballistic missiles. Because of the restraints imposed by Islamabad's limited scientific and industrial base, any Pakistani military missiles almost certainly had to be developed from foreign components with external technical assistance, or be obtained as a

---

[235] Ibid

[236] Ibid

[237] JDW, India pressured to halt Prithvi productions, April 1995, Pg5

[238] Ibid

[239] Eric Arnett, Military Capacity and the Risk of War- China, India, Pakistan and Iran, Oxford University Press, 1997, Pg268

[240] JDW, Prithvi put back in production, 7 October, 1995, Pg17

[241] JDW, Asia's missiles race hots up, 1994, Pg20

[242] Ibid

[243] Ibid

complete missile system package. However, Pakistan has consolidated its limited experience in this avenue, and has also used unconventional means to acquire the technology for its ballistic missile programme in order to counter an ascending Indian threat.[244]

Islamabad's attempts to indigenously develop ballistic missiles have been slow. Some uncertainty surrounds the exact designations of Islamabad's various missile systems due to its close co-operation with Beijing. Two missile systems were initially indigenously developed: the Hatf-1 and the Hatf-2, with ranges of 80 km and 300 km respectively. Despite their ability to carry a 500 kg payload, these missiles have a very poor circular error of probability (CEP).[245]

The failure to induct the indigenously developed Hatf I and II missiles has meant that the Pakistan government looked elsewhere for the technology to counter the Prithvi missiles. China has helped Pakistan, offering Pakistan the blueprint designs and manufacturing infrastructure required to build the M-11 ballistic missile. The production of the M-11 at Rawalpindi, which is capable of carrying a nuclear warhead to a range of 280 km, adds to the 30 M-11 missiles Islamabad received from China in 1992.[246]

Pakistan had developed the Ghauri missile, with a range of 1,500 km, in response to India's resumption of the Agni intermediate-range ballistic missile programme, putting New Delhi, Bombay and Madras within Ghauri's range. In the short-term, Pakistan's M-11 missile has a two-to-one range advantage over India's Prithvi I. (However, Pakistan's population centres are closer to the border than are India's which leaves Pakistan in a more vulnerable situation).[247] By 2018, Pakistan now produces a sophisticated range of ballistic missiles, such as the Shaheen 3 and the Ababeel MIRV missiles.

The latest purchase of the Russian SU-30 strike-aircraft, in addition to the existing squadrons of MIG-27s, Mirage-2000s and Jaguars have considerably enhanced Indian strike capabilities. According to Dr. Eric Arnett of the Stockholm International Peace Research Institute (SIPRI), the arms sales consisting of heavy laser-guided bombs and related equipment have been sold to the Indian Air Force over the past decade by Russia, Britain, America and Israel. These sophisticated arms have increased Pakistan's dependency on its range of ballistic missiles, such as the Ghauri missile etc., which is intended for deployment along the border with India.

"These weapons can destroy Pakistan's nuclear delivery systems even in hardened shelters. The Pakistan's Air Force's fear about the vulnerability of its aircraft must have been one of the main factors in the decision to develop and test the Ghauri ballistic missile".[248]

The development of ballistic missiles, with a delivery time of under three minutes, has raised the dilemma for both countries to use "use or lose" their nuclear weapons in an escalating crisis. Both nations might perceive the need for a 'first-strike' policy, to pre-empt the other side. There is an evident risk of lower-level officials in the field to seize the nuclear initiative without orders from the central government, due to the almost complete absence of command-and control centres at present. This instability is also exacerbated by the lack of early warning systems, or false-alarm contingencies, and also because speed of an attack would render any possible contingency ineffective.[249]

The disputed territory of Kashmir has the potential to trigger the next 'Cuban Missile Crisis'. Unknown to the Kennedy Administration in 1962, Soviet field commanders were authorised to launch nuclear missiles if the United States attacked Cuba. Given the absence of warning, the same is likely to be true of Indian and Pakistani military commanders in the vicinity of Kashmir. However, given the fact that India and Pakistan share common borders, the potential for a nuclear disaster appears much greater than any during the Cold War.[250]

Overall Nuclear delivery systems

A list of India's potential nuclear delivery vehicles is provided here. The nuclear weapons potential of India's

---

[244] Ibid

[245] Ibid

[246] JDW, USA links Chinese ties to missile Exports, 1994, Pg6

[247] Ibid

[248] Eric Arnett, Delhi able to play nuclear trump in game for control of Kashmir, The Times, May 1998, Pg21

[249] Greenville, op cit:593

[250] Ibid

estimated fissile material stocks will be equivalent to 130 warheads by the end of 2017.

India, Possible Nuclear Delivery Vehicles, 2018

AIRCRAFT				
Type-	Number Deployed	Range (Km)	Payload (Kg)	Speed
Jaguar	117	2,600	4,750	Mach 1.5
Mig-27	65	1,100	4,000	Mach 1.7
Mig-29	63	1,500	3,000	Mach 2.35
Su-30MKI	250	3,000	8,000	Mach 2.0
Mirage 2000	50	1,850	6,300	Mach 2.2

Land-Based Missiles				
Type-	Number Deployed	Range (Km)	Payload (Kg)	Classification
Prithvi-150	Operational	150	1,000	BSRBM
Prithvi-250	Operational	250	500	SRBM
Prithvi-350	Operational	350	500	SRBM
Agni 1	Operational	700	1,000	MRBM
Agni 2/3/4	Tested/Dev	2,500-4,000	1,000	IRBM

| Agni 5 | Tested/Dev | 5,000-8,000 | Unknown | ICBM |

Submarine-Launched Ballistic Missiles

Type-	Number Deployed	Range (Km)	Payload (Kg)	Classification
Sagarika	Tested/Dev	700-750	500	SLBM
Shaurya	Tested/Dev	3,000-3,500	500	SLBM

Source: federation of American scientists, Centre for Defence Information, PIADS intelligence Unit[251]

India's Nuclear capable aircraft

Jaguar

Jaguar is a dedicated attack/strike aircraft of the IAF

MIG-27 Flogger

Mig-27 Flogger – primary attack aircraft in the IAF

---

[251] Centre for Defence Information (Internet)

MIG-29 Fulcrum

Su-30MKI Flanker

Mirage 2000

LCA Tejas

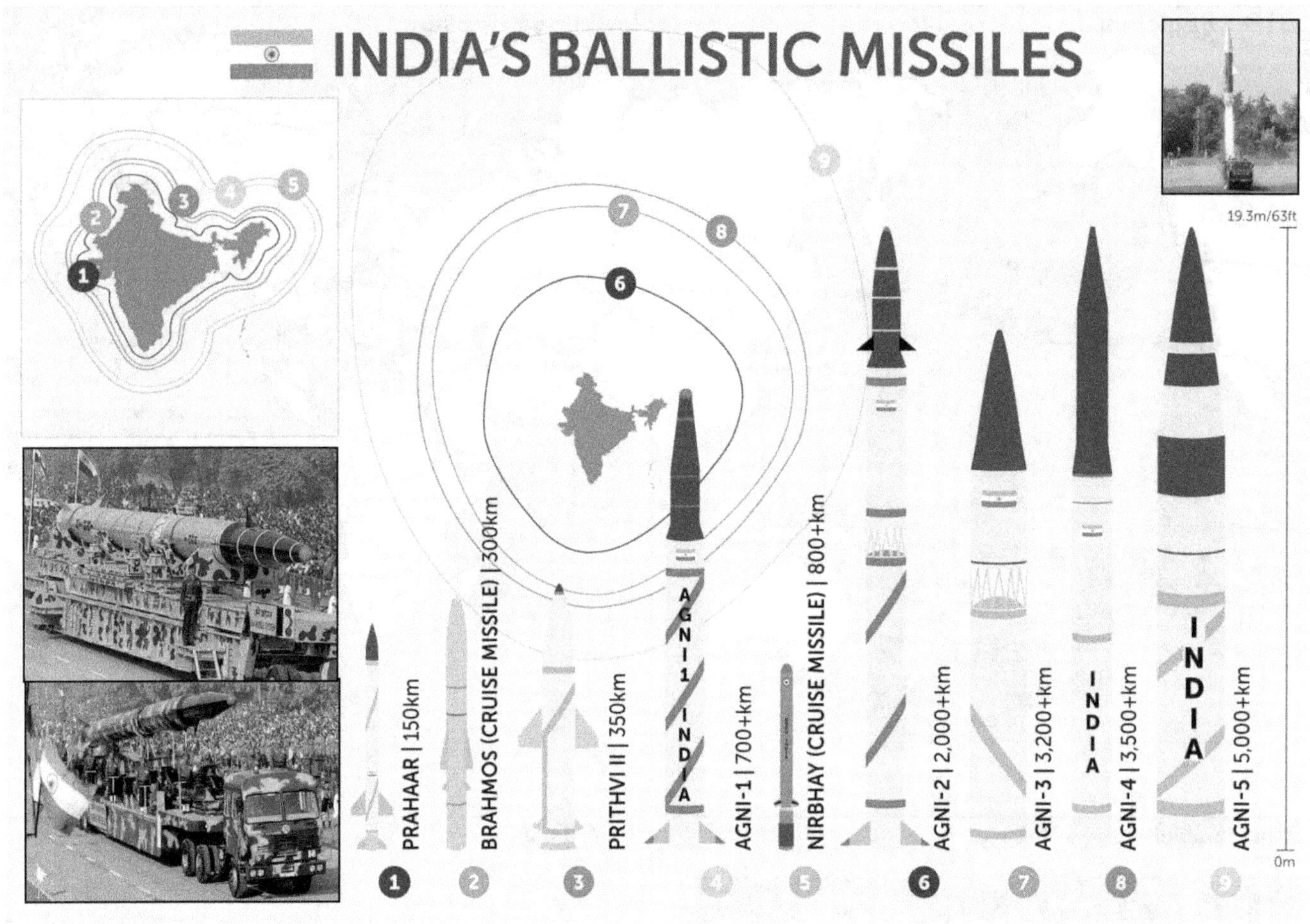

INDIA'S BALLISTIC MISSILES

Agni-5

Originated from: India
Possessed by: India
Class: Intercontinental Ballistic Missile (ICBM)
Basing: Road-mobile

Length: 17.5-20 m
Diameter: 2.0-2.2 m
Launch weight: 49,000-55,000 kg
Warhead: Unknown
Propulsion: Three-stage solid propellant
Range: 5,000-8,000 km
Status: Development
Tested: 2013

The Agni-5 is India's developing ICBM program,

Agni-4

Originated from: India
Possessed by: India
Class: Intermediate-Range Ballistic Missile (IRBM)
Length: 20.0 m
Launch weight: 17,000 kg
Payload: Single warhead, 800 kg
Warhead: Nuclear 20 or 45 kT, Fusion 200-300 kT
Propulsion: Two-stage solid propellant
Range: 3,500-4,000 km

Status: In development
In service: N/A

The Agni-4 is a two-stage solid propellant missile with a length of 20.0 m and a launch weight of 17,000 kg. Reports suggest that the Agni-4 can be fitted with a 20 or 45 kT nuclear warhead, or a 200-300 kT fusion warhead.

The Agni-4 is road mobile and carried by a truck TEL,

which consists of a three stage solid fueled missile potentially with MIRVed warheads. Though the missile has only been tested out to 5,000 km, classifying it as an intermediate range missile, news reports and officials consistently refer to the missile as an ICBM, potentially suggesting an extended range.[252]

unlike the Agni-3, which is primarily rail-mobile. The missile uses a combination of a ring laser gyro-based inertial navigation system and a redundant micro inertial navigation system for guidance, giving it double digit CEP.[253]

Agni-3

Originated from: India
Possessed by: India
Class: Intermediate-Range Ballistic Missile (IRBM)
Basing: Rail-mobile, possible road-based TEL
Length: 16.7 m
Diameter: 1.85 m
Launch weight: 48,000 kg
Payload: Single warhead, 2,000 kg
Warhead: Nuclear fusion 200-300 kT; possible MIRV version
Propulsion: 2-stage solid propellant
Range: 3,000-5,000 km
Status: Operational

The maximum payload of the Agni-3 is 2,000 kg. Some suggest a fusion warhead of about 200-300 kT will be the primary warhead and others claim the missile could carry MIRVs, conventional high explosives, or submunitions. The RV likely uses an imaging infrared or active radar terminal correlation seeker, reported to have an accuracy of 40 m CEP.

Rail-based launchers have exclusively fired the Agni-3 so far, though reports suggest future development of a truck TEL for a road-mobile version as well. In 2014, the Indian Ministry of Defense declared the Agni-3 part of the arsenal of the armed forces and the missile was part of its third user trial in April 2015.[254]

Agni-2

Originated from: India
Possessed by: India
Alternate name: Agni-II
Class: Medium-Range Ballistic Missile
Basing: Road/rail-mobile
Length: 20.0 m
Diameter: 1.30 m
Launch weight: 16,000 kg
Payload: Single warhead, 1,000 kg
Warhead: Nuclear 150 kt or 200kt, HE
Propulsion: Two-stage solid propellant
Range: 2,000-3,500 km
Status: Operational
In service: 2004

The Agni-2 is a two-stage, medium-range, rail/road-mobile, solid propellant ballistic missile. In its present configuration, the missile is 20 m in length with a diameter of 1.3 m in the first and second stages. The missile carries a warhead weighing up to 1,000 kg usually consisting of either 150 or 200 kT yield nuclear warheads, but also potentially high-explosive conventional versions. The Agni-2 uses a combination of inertial navigation and GPS in its guidance module as well as dual-frequency radar correlation for terminal guidance. Older Agni-2 models used four moving control fins in order to maneuver independently during the terminal phase. Newer models use side thrust motors instead. It has been reported to have an accuracy of 40 m CEP.[255]

---

[252] Agni-5 - https://missilethreat.csis.org/missile/agni-5/

[253] Agni-4 - https://missilethreat.csis.org/missile/agni-4/

[254] Agni-3 - https://missilethreat.csis.org/missile/agni-3/

[255] Agni-2 - https://missilethreat.csis.org/missile/agni-2/

Agni-1

Originated from: India
Possessed by: India
Class: Short-Range Ballistic Missile (SRBM)
Basing: Road/rail-mobile
Length: 14.80 m
Diameter: 1.30 m
Launch weight: 12,000 kg
Payload: Single warhead, 2,000 kg
Warhead: Nuclear 20 or 45 kT, HE, submunitions, FAE
Propulsion: Single-stage solid propellant
Range: 700-1,200 km
Status: Operational
In service: 2004

The Agni-1 is a short-range, road/rail-mobile, solid propellant ballistic missile. Falling between the short-range and medium-range categories, it fills the gap between India's Prithvi systems and the Agni-2.

The Agni-1 is 14.8 m long, 1.3 m in diameter, with a launch weight of 12,000 kg. It has a range of 700 km with an accuracy of 25 m CEP at a range of 860 km. At its maximum payload of 2,000 kg, the missile can carry a 20 or 45 kT nuclear warhead, or conventional explosives.[256]

Sagarika / Shaurya

Originated from: India
Possessed by: India
Class: Short-Range Ballistic Missile (SRBM)/Medium-Range Ballistic Missile (MRBM)
Basing: sub-launched
Length: 10.8 m (Sagarika), 12 m (Shaurya)
Diameter: 0.8 m
Propulsion: Two-stage solid propellant
Range: 700-750 km (Sagarika), 3,000-3,500 km (Shaurya)

Sagarika

The Indian sub-launched ballistic missile (SLBM) program began in the 1990's. Work on an Indian SLBM likely began with the Sagarika or K-15/B-05 program, which has now given way to the K-4 or Shaurya program.

Sagarika

The Sagarika has a maximum range of 700 km and is powered by a two-stage solid propellant motor. It has a reported length of 10.8 m, a body diameter of 0.8 m, and a launch weight of 5,500 to 6,300 kg. The payload can be HE or nuclear with a weight of 500 to 800 kg. It uses Inertial Navigation System and Global Positioning System with terrain contour matching in the terminal phase.

Shaurya

Early testing of the Shaurya happened on land, with many suggesting that it was the land-based version of the Sagarika after tests in 2008 and 2011. The missile underwent its first undersea launch in March 2014 from a submerged barge, also demonstrating an expanded range of 3,000 km. The missile was tested again, firing at a depressed trajectory from an undersea barge and allegedly to a range of 3,500 km. The missile has already been tested from the Arihant. It is likely that the missile is intended to carry a nuclear payload to complete India's nuclear triad of delivery vehicles and could likely be outfitted with other conventional payloads.[257]

---

[256] Agni-1 - https://missilethreat.csis.org/missile/agni-1/

[257] Sagarika/Shaurya - https://missilethreat.csis.org/missile/sagarika-shaurya/

Prithvi-I/II/III

Originated from: India
Possessed by: India
Alternate names: P-1, P-2, P-3
Class: Short-Range Ballistic Missile (SRBM)
Basing: Ground-launched
Status: Operational
In service: 1994

The Prithvi class of ballistic missiles make up most of India's arsenal of short-range ballistic missiles, useful for more tactical and battlefield uses. All of the missiles are road-mobile, allowing them to be deployed with maneuvering forces. The missiles have steadily improved their range from the 150 km Prithvi-I to the 350 km Prithvi-III and have progressed from liquid fueled to solid fueled over the same progression.[258]

Dhanush

Originated from: India
Possessed by: India

Class: Short-Range Ballistic Missile (SRBM)
Basing: Ship-launched
Length: 8.53 m
Diameter: 1.0 m
Launch weight: 5600 kg
Payload: Single warhead, 500-1000 kg
Warhead: Nuclear, HE, submunitions, FAE, or chemical
Propulsion: Single-stage liquid propellant
Range: 250-400 km
Status: Operational
In service: 2010

The Dhanush missile is a short-range, ship-based ballistic missile – probably with a liquid propellant base – that is the naval version of India's Prithvi missile. The payload is presumed to be 500 to 1000 kg, with various warhead options including HE, submunitions, FAE, or chemical. It is powered by a single-stage liquid propellant and guided by an inertial system or GPS. The range is estimated in between 150 and 400 km, with an accuracy of 50 m CEP. Some sources suggest the accuracy is 25 m CEP.[259]

BrahMos

Originated from: Russia and India
Possessed by: Russia, India, Vietnam
Alternate names: PJ-10
Class: Supersonic Cruise Missile
Length: 8.0-8.2 m
Diameter: 0.67 m
Launch weight: 2,200-3,000 kg
Payload: 200-300 kg
Warhead: HE, submunitions

Prahaar

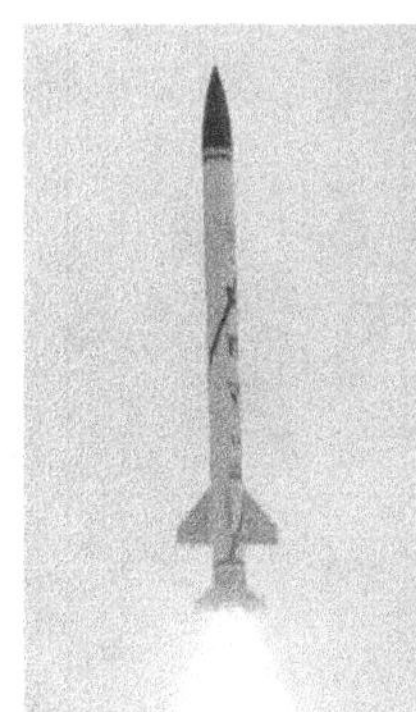

Originated from: India
Possessed by: India
Class: Short-Range Ballistic Missile (SRBM)
Basing: Road-mobile
Length: 7.3 m
Diameter: 0.42 m
Launch Weight: 1,280 kg
Payload: Single warhead, 200 kg
Warhead: Nuclear, HE, submunitions
Propulsion: Single-stage solid propellant
Range: 150 km

The Prahaar is a short-range, solid propellant, road-mobile ballistic missile designed for tactical strikes against close

---

[258] Prithvi-I/II/III - https://missilethreat.csis.org/missile/prithvi/

[259] Dhanush - https://missilethreat.csis.org/missile/dhanush/

Propulsion: Liquid-fueled ramjet
Range: 300-500 km, 290 km export version
Basing: Ground-launched, Air-launched, Sub-launched, Ship-launched
Status: Operational

The BrahMos (PJ-10) is a short-range, ramjet powered, single warhead, supersonic anti-ship/land attack cruise missile developed and manufactured by India and Russia The BrahMos has a reported supersonic speed of between Mach 2.0-2.8, depending on the cruising altitude used. It has the stealth capability to evade radars and other detection methods, having greater strike power. It has an inertial navigation system (INS) for use against ship targets, and an INS/Global Positioning System for use against land targets. Terminal guidance is achieved through an active/passive radar.[260]

range targets.

The missile has a length of 7.3 m, a body diameter of 0.42 m, and a launch weight of 1,280 kg. It can carry a 200 kg payload with planned nuclear, HE, and submunition options. It can travel up to 150 km and is propelled by a single-stage solid propellant engine. The Prahaar is carried by the TATRA Transporter-Erector-Launcher vehicle and can hold six missiles per truck. Each missile is believed to be vertically launched, and they can be launched in salvo mode for multiple azimuth attacks.[261]

Nirbhay

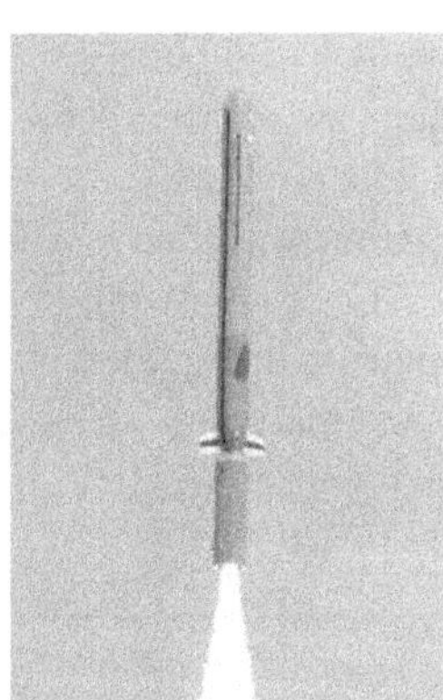

Originated from: India
Possessed by: India
Class: Subsonic Cruise Missile
Length: 6.0 m
Diameter: 0.5 m
Launch weight: 1,500-1,6000 kg
Payload: 450 kg
Warhead: HE, submunitions, 12 kT nuclear potentially
Propulsion: Turbojet
Range: 800-1,000 km

The missile uses a solid propellant booster motor that is jettisoned shortly after launch, switching over to a turbojet engine with a cruise speed of 0.65 Mach and a reported range of 800-1,000 km. The missile is guided by INS/GPS with an active-radar terminal seeker, and its accuracy could be improved both by the development of an indigenous Indian navigation satellite system and the potential of integrating the seeker from the BrahMos missile, which could be tested in December 2016.[262]

---

[260] BrahMos - https://missilethreat.csis.org/missile/brahmos/

[261] Prahaar - https://missilethreat.csis.org/missile/prahaar/

[262] Nirbhay - https://missilethreat.csis.org/missile/nirbhay/

A list of Pakistan's potential nuclear delivery vehicles is provided here. The nuclear weapons potential of Pakistan's estimated fissile material stock is 140 warheads by the end of 2017.

Pakistan, Possible Nuclear Delivery Vehicles, 2018

AIRCRAFT				
Type-	**Number Deployed**	**Range (Km)**	**Payload (Kg)**	**Classification**
JF-17 Thunder	85	600	3,500	Mach 1.12
Mirage III/5	171	500	3,500	Mach 2.2
F-16	76	850	2,500	Mach 2
Land-Based Missiles				
Type-	**Number Deployed**	**Range (Km)**	**Payload (Kg)**	**Classification**
M-11	Storage (40-84)	280	800	SRBM
Hatf 9 Nasr	Operational	60-70	500	BSRBM
Hatf 1/A	Operational	70-100	500	BSRBM
Hatf 2 Abdali	Operational	180-200	500	SRBM
Hatf 3 Ghaznavi	Operational	290	500	SRBM
Shaheen 1/2	Operational	750-2,000	500	MRBM
Hatf 5 Ghauri	Operational	1,250-1,500	500-750	MRBM

Shaheen 3	Tested/Dev	2,750	Unknown	MRBM
Ababeel	Tesyted/Dev	2,200	Unknown	IRBM
Babur (GLCM)	Operational	350-700	500	MRBM
		Submarine Launched Cruise Missile (SLCM)		
Babur 3 (SLCM)	Tested/Dev	450-700	500	MRBM

Source: federation of American scientists, Centre for Defence Information, PIADS intelligence Unit[263]

CLASSIFICATIONS OF BALLISTIC MISSILES BY RANGE

BSRB M	Battlefield Short Range	Upto 150km	Up to 94 miles
SRBM	Short Range	150-699km	94-499 miles
MRB M	Medium Range	700-2,499km	500-1,499 miles
		2,500-5,499km	1,500-3,437 miles
IRBM	Intermediate Range	5,499km	
ICBM	Intercontinental	+5,000km	+3,438 miles
SLBM	Submarine Launched		No specific Range Classification

Pakistan's Nuclear capable aircraft

Mirage III/5	**F-16 Fighting Falcon**

---

[263] Centre for Defence Information (Internet)

JF-17 Thunder

JF-17 Thunder combat aircraft

Pakistan's most sophisticated type – the US F-16 Falcon Multi-role combat aircraft

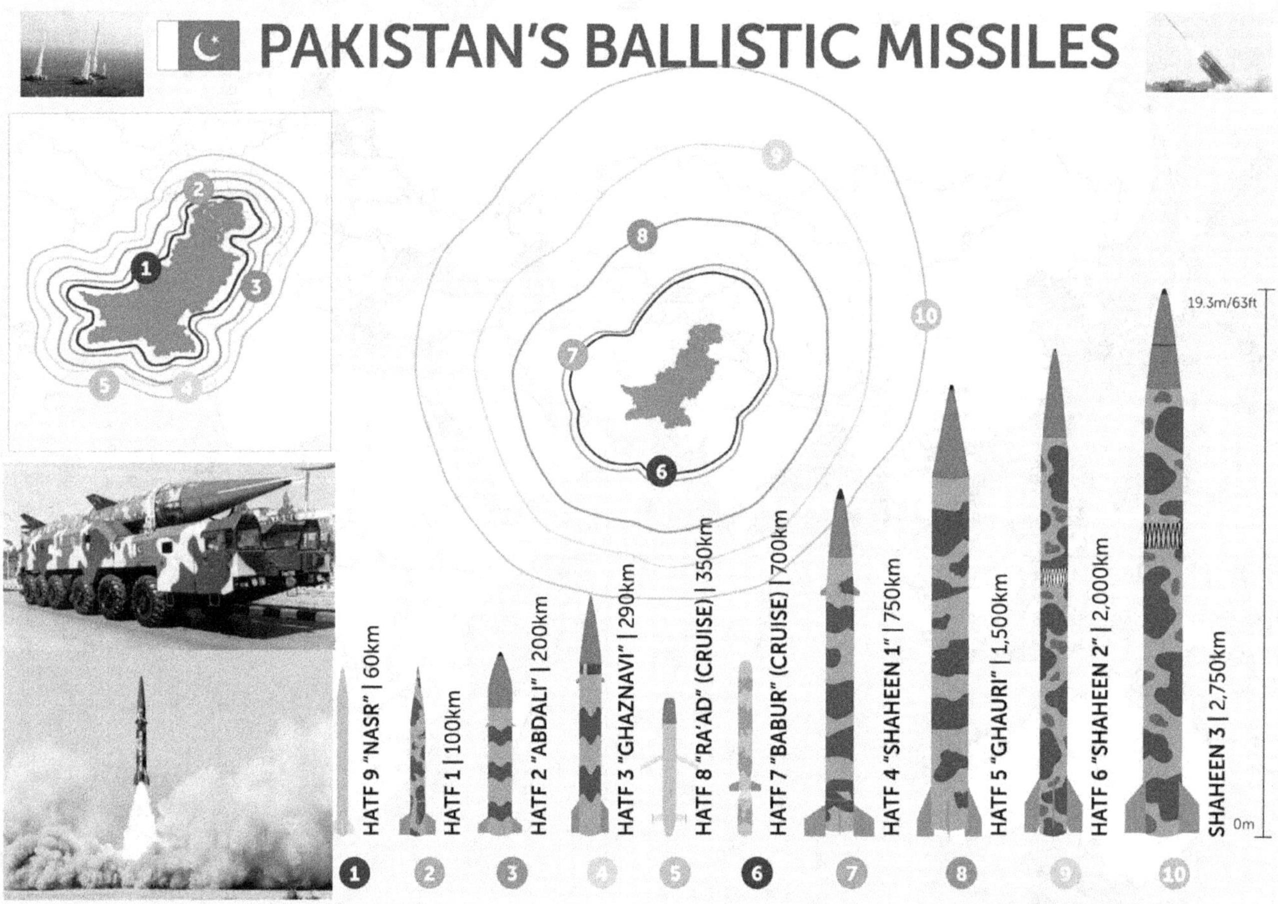

Missiles of Pakistan - Center for Strategic and International Studies (CSIS)[264]

[264] Missiles of Pakistan, Center for Strategic and International Studies (CSIS) - https://missilethreat.csis.org/country/pakistan/?lcp_page0=1#lcp_instance_0

Ababeel (MIRV)

Originated from: Pakistan
Possessed by: Pakistan
Class: Medium-range ballistic missile
Basing: Road-mobile
Length: Unknown
Diameter: 1.7 m (est.)
Warhead: Nuclear, Conventional
Payload: Multiple Independently Targetable Re-Entry Vehicle
Propulsion: Solid-fuel
Range: 2,200 km
Status: In development
In Service: N/A
Tested: January 24, 2017

The Ababeel is Pakistan's first surface-to-surface medium range ballistic missile (MRBM), reportedly capable of carrying Multiple Independently Targetable Re-entry Vehicles (MIRVs). The Ababeel is a three-stage, solid-fuel medium-range ballistic missile with a reported maximum range of 2,200 km[265]

Shaheen 3 (MRBM)

Originated from: Pakistan
Possessed by: Pakistan
Class: Medium-Range Ballistic Missile (MRBM)
Basing: Road-mobile
Length: 19.3 m
Diameter: 1.4 m
Payload: Nuclear, conventional
Propulsion: Two-stage, Solid-propellant
Range: 2,750 km
Status: In development
Tested: March, December 2015

The Shaheen 3 missile is a two-stage, solid-fueled medium-range ballistic missile in development by Pakistan. The missile is reportedly capable of carrying both nuclear and conventional payloads to a range of 2,750 km, which would make it the longest range missile in Pakistan's strategic arsenal. It was first publicly displayed during a military parade in March 2016. The Shaheen 3 is road-mobile and reportedly mounted on a Chinese transporter erector launcher.[266]

Hatf 9 Nasr

Originated from: Pakistan
Possessed by: Pakistan
Alternate name: Nasr
Class: Short-Range Ballistic Missile (SRBM)
Basing: Road-mobile
Length: 6 m
Diameter: 0.4 m
Launch weight: 1,200 kg
Payload: Single warhead, 400 kg
Warhead: Nuclear, HE, submunitions
Propulsion: Single-stage solid propellant
Range: 60 km
Status: In development
Tested: April 2011

Hatf 8 Ra'ad

Originated from: Pakistan
Possessed by: Pakistan
Class: Subsonic Cruise Missile
Basing: Air-launched
Length: 4.85 m
Diameter: 0.5 m
Warhead: HE, nuclear, conventional
Propulsion: Turbojet
Range: 350 km
Status: Unknown

Tests of the Ra'ad have been largely conducted from Pakistan's Mirage III fighter jets, but there is potential for future systems such as the JF-17 fighter that could also host the Ra'ad. The Ra'ad has the given Pakistan a stand-off capability because it can deliver both nuclear and conventional payloads to a target from a 350 km range over and above the maximum range of the aircraft.

---

[265] Ababeel MIRV - https://missilethreat.csis.org/missile/ababeel/

[266] Shaheen 3 - https://missilethreat.csis.org/missile/shaheen-3/

The Hatf 9 Nasr is a Pakistani surface-to-surface short-range ballistic missile. The Hatf 9 is also believed to be a nuclear capable missile, but it could potentially carry an HE or submunitions payload as well.[267]	Pakistani media reports the Ra'ad to be a "low-altitude, terrain hugging missile with high maneuverability" as well as "stealth capabilities [and] pinpoint accuracy."[268]

Hatf 7 Babur	Hatf 6 Shaheen 2
 **Originated from:** Pakistan **Possessed by:** Pakistan **Class:** Subsonic Cruise Missile **Basing:** Ground launched **Length:** 6.2 m **Diameter:** 0.52 m **Launch weight:** 1,500 kg **Payload:** Single warhead, 450-500 kg, nuclear capable **Warhead:** 10-35 kT nuclear, HE, submunitions **Propulsion:** Turbojet **Range:** 350-700 km **Status:** Operational **In service:** 2010-present **Tested:** August 2005 **The Hatf 7 Babur** is a short-range, turbojet-powered ground-launch cruise missile. The Hatf 7 is estimated to have a length of 6.2 m, a diameter of 0.52 m, and fold-out wings with a 2.5 m wingspan. With a launch weight around 1,500 kg, it is capable of carrying a 450 kg payload up to 700 km. The missile can be equipped with either a single 10 or 35 kT nuclear warhead, or up to 450 kg worth of conventional explosives (HE unitary or submunitions.[269]	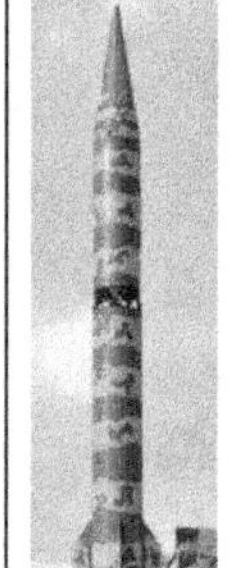 **Originated from:** Pakistan **Possessed by:** Pakistan **Class:** Medium-Range Ballistic Missile (MRBM) **Basing:** Road-mobile **Length:** 17.2 m **Diameter:** 1.4 m **Launch weight:** 23,600 kg **Payload:** Single warhead, 700 kg **Warhead:** 15-35 kT nuclear, HE, submunitions, chemical **Propulsion:** Two-stage solid propellant **Range:** 1,500-2,000 km **Status:** Operational **In service:** 2014-present **Tested:** August 2005 The Shaheen 2 has a reported range of between 1,500-2,000 km. It is designed to carry a single warhead payload weighing 700 kg, though reports suggest that payloads up to 1,230 kg have been developed. Increasing the payload weight, however, may shorten the missile's range. The Hatf 6 warhead can be equipped for a nuclear yield between 15 and 35 kT. There are also provisions to deploy the missile with conventional high explosives (HE), submunitions, fuel-air explosives (FAE), or chemical agents. It is launched from a transporter-erector-launcher (TEL). [270]

---

267 Hatf 9 Nasr - https://missilethreat.csis.org/missile/hatf-9/

268 Hatf 8 Ra'ad - https://missilethreat.csis.org/missile/hatf-8/

269 Hatf 7 Babur - https://missilethreat.csis.org/missile/hatf-7/

270 Hatf 6 Shaheen 2 - https://missilethreat.csis.org/missile/hatf-6/

Hatf 5 Ghauri

Originated from: North Korea / Pakistan
Possessed by: Pakistan
Class: Medium-Range Ballistic Missile (MRBM)
Basing: Road-mobile
Length: 15.9 m
Diameter: 1.35 m
Launch weight: 15,850 kg
Payload: Single warhead, 700 kg +
Warhead: 12-35 kT nuclear, HE, submunitions, chemical
Propulsion: Single-stage liquid propellant
Range: 1,250-1,500 km
Status: Operational
In service: 2003

The Hatf 5 Ghauri is a medium-range, road-mobile, liquid-fueled ballistic missile deployed by Pakistan. It can carry a 700 kg warhead up to 1,500 km. Hatf 5's range and nuclear capability give it the ability to hold targets deep within Indian territory at risk , making it a core part of Pakistan's strategic missile forces.

Hatf 5A (Ghauri 2)

The Ghauri 2 is a medium-range, road-mobile, liquid propellant ballistic missile currently under development. It is a longer ranged variant of the Hatf 5, developed by replacing the heavier steel construction with an aluminum alloy and using improved propellants. It is expected to have a range of at least 1,800 km.[271]

Hatf 4 Shaheen 1

Originated from: China/Pakistan
Possessed by: Pakistan
Class: Short-Range Ballistic Missile (SRBM)
Basing: Road-mobile
Length: 12.0 m
Diameter: 1.0 m
Launch weight: 9,500 kg
Payload: Single warhead, 700 kg
Warhead: 35 kT nuclear, HE, submunitions, chemical
Propulsion: Single-stage solid propellant
Range: 750 km
Status: Operational
In service: 2003-present

The Hatf 4 Shaheen 1 is a short-range, road-mobile, solid-fueled ballistic missile. The Hatf 4 has a range of 750 km when carrying its standard payload and an accuracy of 200 m CEP. Its accuracy is provided by an inertial guidance system, and utilizes a "post separation attitude correction system" which helps increase its accuracy and may give it rudimentary ability to evade missile defense systems. It uses a single-stage, solid propellant engine and can carry a single high-explosive, chemical, or 35 kt nuclear warhead payload weighing up to 1,000 kg. The missile measures 12.0 m in length, 1.0 m in diameter, and has a launch weight of 9,500 kg.[272]

---

[271] Hatf 5 Ghauri - https://missilethreat.csis.org/missile/hatf-5/

[272] Hatf 4 Shaheen 1 - https://missilethreat.csis.org/missile/hatf-4/

Hatf 3 Ghaznavi

Originated from: Pakistan
Possessed by: Pakistan
Class: Short-Range Ballistic Missile (SRBM)
Basing: Road-mobile
Length: 8.5 m
Diameter: 0.8 m
Launch weight: 4,650 kg
Payload: Single warhead, 700 kg
Warhead: HE, submunitions, 12-20 kT nuclear
Propulsion: Single-stage solid propellant
Range: 290 km
Status: Operational
In service: 2004

Hatf-3 appears to be an improved 'Scud' type ballistic missile. Its greatest military utility is in deployment against large, fixed targets such as military bases, airfields, and poses a threat to civilian urban areas. The Hatf 3 is around 8.5 m in length, 0.8 m in diameter, and 4,650 kg in launch weight. It can carry a single warhead up to 700 kg a maximum of 290 km.[273]

Hatf 2 Abdali

Originated from: Pakistan
Possessed by: Pakistan
Class: Short-Range Ballistic Missile (SRBM)
Basing: Road-mobile
Length: 6.5 m
Diameter: 0.56 m
Launch weight: 1,750 kg
Payload: Single warhead, 250-450 kg
Warhead: HE, submunitions, conventional
Propulsion: Single-stage solid propellant
Range: 180-200 km
Status: Operational
In service: 2005

The Hatf 2 Abdali is a short-range, road-mobile, solid propellant missile that entered service in 2005. Hatf 2 is equipped with an inertial guidance system and has a CEP of 150 m. It is estimated to carry a variable payload between 250 and 450 kg that affects its range, which falls between 180 and 200 km, and can carry a single high explosive or submunition warhead. It uses a single-stage solid propellant engine and has a length of 6.5 m and a width of 0.56 m.T he use of solid propellant and the TEL vehicle make the missile easy to store, transport and fire.[274]

Hatf 1 (Vengeance/Deadly missile)

Originated from: Pakistan
Possessed by: Pakistan
Class: Short-Range Ballistic Missile (SRBM)
Basing: Road-mobile

---

[273] Hatf 3 Ghaznavi - https://missilethreat.csis.org/missile/hatf-3/

[274] Hatf 2 Abdali - https://missilethreat.csis.org/missile/hatf-2/

Length: 6.0 m
Diameter: 0.56 m
Launch weight: 1,500 kg
Payload: Single warhead, 500 kg
Warhead: Conventional
Propulsion: Solid propellant
Range: 70-100 km
Status: Operational
In service: 1992

The Hatf 1 is a short-range, road-mobile, solid-fueled ballistic missile. There are three versions: the 1, 1A, and 1B. The Hatf 1 is probably deployed with high explosive or chemical weapons, and although it could theoretically carry a tactical nuclear weapon, Pakistan has declared it to be non-nuclear. The missile is single staged, with a diameter of 0.56 m and is 6 m in length. Due to its solid propellant, it is simple to store, transport, and fire.[275]

Babur-3 Submarine-launched cruise missile (SLCM)

Originated from: Pakistan
Possessed by: Pakistan
Class: Subsonic Cruise Missile
Basing: Submarine-launched cruise missile (SLCM)
Length: 6.2 m
Diameter: 0.52 m
Launch weight: 1,500 kg
Payload: Single warhead, 450-

Harba Surface-to-Surface Anti-ship missile with Land Attack capability (ASCM/LACM)

Originated from: Pakistan
Possessed by: Pakistan
Class: Subsonic Cruise Missile
Basing: Surface-to-Surface Anti-ship missile with Land Attack capability (ASCM/LACM).
Length: 6.2 m
Diameter: 0.52 m
Launch weight: 1,500 kg
Payload: Single warhead, 450-500 kg, nuclear capable

---

[275] Hatf 1 - https://missilethreat.csis.org/missile/hatf-1/

<table>
<tr><td>

500 kg, nuclear capable
Warhead: 10-35 kT nuclear, HE, submunitions
Propulsion: Turbojet
Range: 450-700 km[276]
Status: In development
In service: N/A
Tested: January 9, 2017

Babur 3 is a short-range, turbojet-powered Submarine-launched cruise missile (SLCM). According to ISPR's announcement, the Babur-3 missile, "is capable of delivering various types of payloads and will provide Pakistan with a Credible Second Strike Capability, augmenting deterrence."[277] Babur-3 is thought to have a range of 450 kilometers (some 280 miles) and some analysts have said it was 7oo km.[278] It is said that this SLCM will see Pakistan's nuclear deterrent head to sea—probably initially aboard its Agosta 90B and Agosta 70 submarines, but eventually, perhaps even on board new Type 041 *Yuan*-class submarines Pakistan is expected to procure from China.[279]

</td><td>

Warhead: 10-35 kT nuclear, HE, submunitions
Propulsion: Turbojet
Range: 450-700 km[280]
Status: In development
In service: N/A
Tested: January 9, 2017

Harba is a short-range, turbojet-powered Surface-to-Surface Anti-ship missile with Land Attack capability (ASCM/LACM). It is thought to be a 'Babur' cruise missile variant. According to the Pakistan Navy, the Harba Naval Cruise Missile is a surface-to-surface anti-ship missile with Land Attack capability. Harba is thought to have a range of 450-700 kilometers. It can also provide long range anti-ship and land attack capability and may add to Pakistan's nuclear deterrence (2nd Strike capability).[281]

</td></tr>
<tr><td>

Taimur Intercontinental Ballistic Missiles (ICBM)

Originated from: Pakistan
Possessed by: Pakistan
Class: Intercontinental Ballistic Missiles (ICBM)
Basing: Road-mobile
Length: Unknown
Diameter: Unknown
Warhead: Nuclear, Conventional
Payload: Single warhead/Multiple Independently Targetable Re-Entry Vehicle
Propulsion: Solid-fuel
Range: 7,000+ km
Status: In development

</td><td>

Tipu Sultan Intercontinental Ballistic Missiles (ICBM)

Originated from: Pakistan
Possessed by: Pakistan
Class: Intercontinental Ballistic Missiles (ICBM)
Basing: Road-mobile
Length: Unknown
Diameter: Unknown
Warhead: Nuclear, Conventional
Payload: Single warhead/Multiple Independently Targetable Re-Entry Vehicle
Propulsion: Solid-fuel
Range: 8,000 – 15000 km

</td></tr>
</table>

---

[276] South Asia's nuclear one-upmanship ramps up with Pakistan missile test - https://edition.cnn.com/2017/01/10/asia/pakistan-submarine-missile/index.html

[277] Safer at Sea? Pakistan's Sea Based Deterrent and Nuclear Weapons Security - https://twq.elliott.gwu.edu/sites/g/files/zaxdzs2121/f/downloads/40-3_ClaryPanda.pdf

[278] Pakistan Conducts 1st Successful Test of Submarine-Launched Cruise Missile - https://sputniknews.com/military/201701091049403419-pakistan-test-missile-sub/

[279] The Risks of Pakistan's Sea-Based Nuclear Weapons - https://thediplomat.com/2017/10/the-risks-of-pakistans-sea-based-nuclear-weapons/

[280] South Asia's nuclear one-upmanship ramps up with Pakistan missile test - https://edition.cnn.com/2017/01/10/asia/pakistan-submarine-missile/index.html

[281] Pakistan Test-fires Harba Anti-Ship Cruise Missile - https://quwa.org/2018/01/03/pakistan-test-fires-harba-anti-ship-cruise-missile/

<table>
<tr><td>

Rumours[282] are stating that Pakistan is developing the Taimur missile[283], with a range of 7,000 km, is an ICBM under development. [284]

</td><td>

Status: In development

Rumours[285] are stating that Pakistan is developing the Tipu Sultan missile, with a range of 7,000 - 15000 km[286], is an ICBM under development.[287]

</td></tr>
</table>

Pakistani ballistic missiles

Pakistan Army Shaheen 3 nuclear capable ballistic missile

---

[282] Know more about Pakistan's most powerful missile Taimur - https://www.indiatvnews.com/news/world/know-more-about-pakistan-s-most-powerful-missile-taimur-14772.html

[283] Intercontinental Ballistic Missile OF Pakistan - http://f9view.com/intercontinental-ballistic-missile-of-pakistan

[284] Arms Control and Proliferation Profile: Pakistan - https://www.armscontrol.org/print/3201

[285] Deterence and Second Strike Capability of South Asia, Centre for Strategic and Contemporary Research (CSCR) - https://cscr.pk/explore/themes/defense-security/deterrence-second-strike-capability-south-asia/

[286] Tipu Sultan 15000 Km - https://www.facebook.com/permalink.php?id=1456469827937711&story_fbid=1458069467777747

[287] China helping Pak with ICBM: U.S. Congressman - http://www.thehindu.com/news/international/china-helping-pak-with-icbm-us-congressman/article8535575.ece

Nuclear TRIAD Complete - Babur-3 Submarine-launched cruise missile (SLCM)

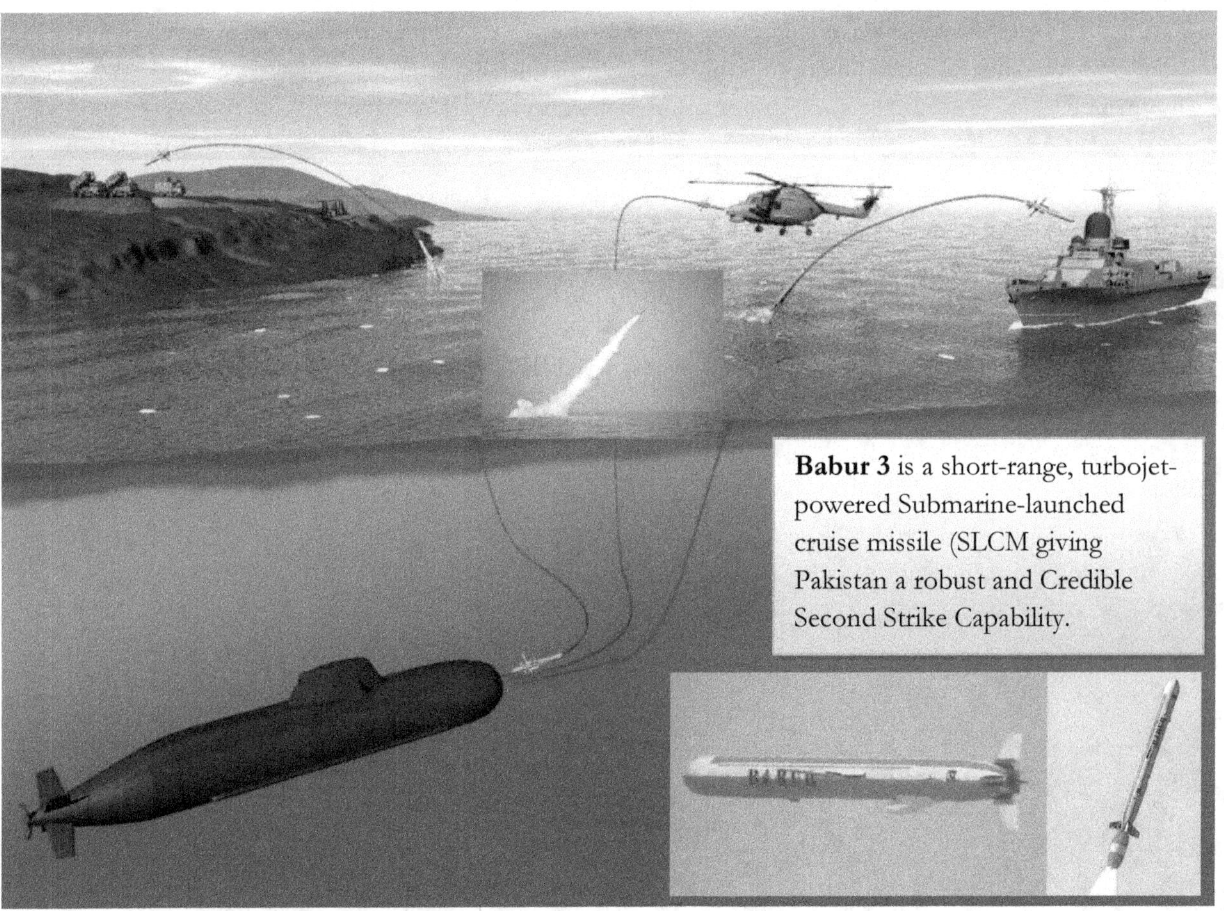

The Babur-3 cruise missile was fired from an underwater, mobile platform and hit its target with precise accuracy (thought to be Pakistan Navy's Agosta class submarines) in a test undertaken on the 9th of January 2017. The Babur-3 SLCM (submarine-launched cruise missile) with a range of 450 - 700 kilometers in land-attack mode is capable of delivering various types of payloads and will provide Pakistan with a credible second strike capability. This should enhance Pakistan's deterrence to any would be adversary.

The Pakistan armed forces had set up Strategic Forces Command and had equipped the army and air force with nuclear weapons (delivery by missiles or aircraft). The Naval Stategic Forces command was lacking in this area, but with the advent of the Babur 3 SLCM this area has been given the capability. The successful testing of Babur-3 SLCM has given the Naval Strategic Force Command its nuclear-capable weapons.[288] This will complete Pakistan's quest for a TRIAD capability that will augment its deterrence capabilities. The second strike capability allows it to strike an adversary after receiveng a first strike from a hostile nation.[289]

---

[288] Pakistan fires nuclear-capable missile from submarine in the Indian Ocean (2017) Kerry B. Collison Asia News - http://kerrycollison.blogspot.co.uk/2017/01/pakistan-fires-nuclear-capable-missile.html

[289] Pakistan completes nuclear triad, launches missile Babur-3 from submarine - http://zeenews.india.com/asia/pakistan-completes-nuclear-triad-launches-missile-babur-3-from-submarine_1965794.html

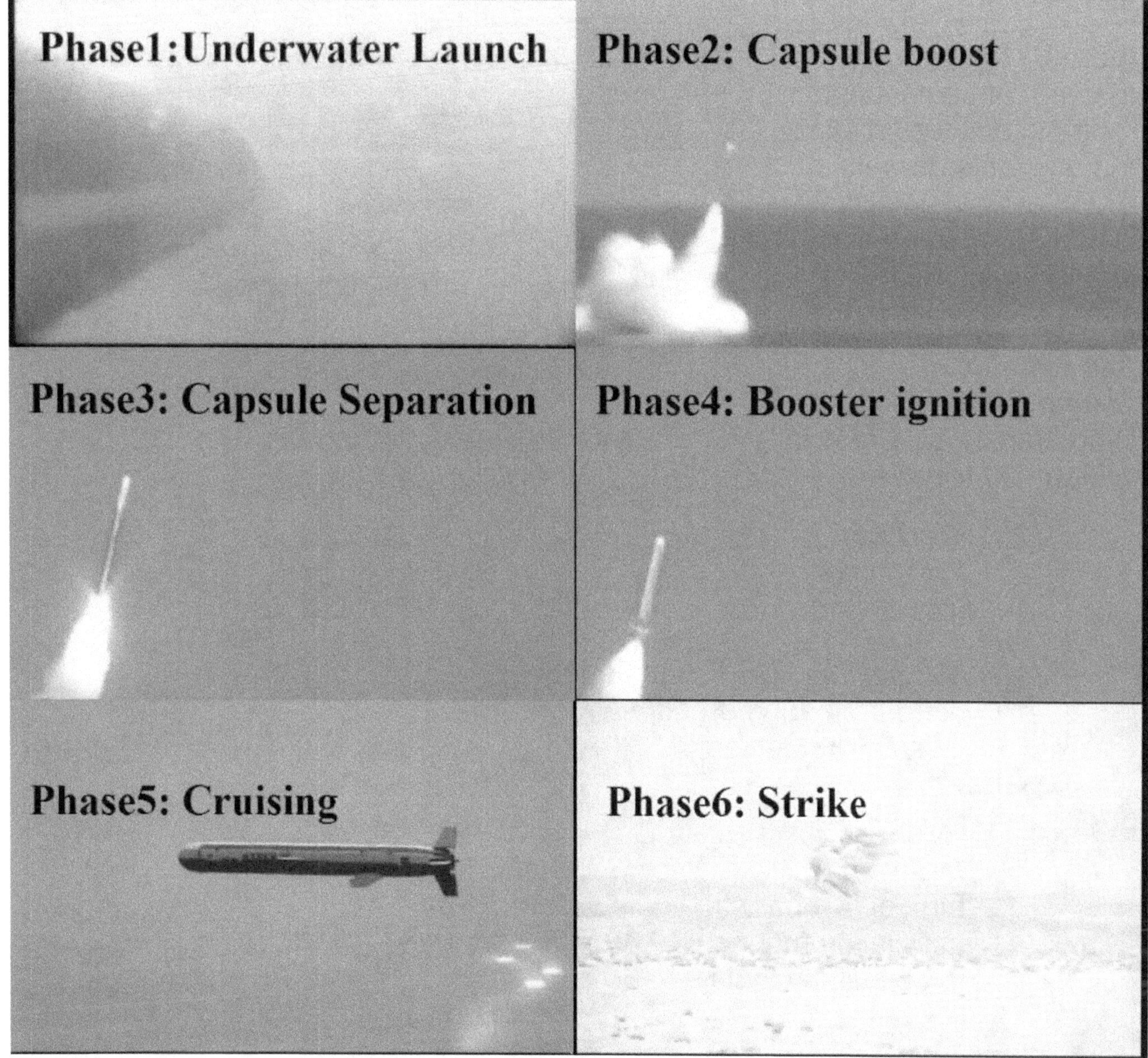

Pakistan on Thursday (29/03/2018) conducted another successful test fire of indigenously developed Submarine Launched Cruise Missile Babur, having a range of 450 kms[290]

Indian TRIAD forces

India has also completed its TRIAD capability where all its 3 services are able launch nuclear weapons by land, air and sea.

---

[290] Pakistan achieves 'credible second strike capability' with successful test of cruise missile Babur - https://www.thenews.com.pk/latest/298244-pakistan-successfully-test-fires-submarine-launched-cruise-missile-babur https://defence.pk/pdf/threads/pakistan-navy-news-discussions.41/page-141

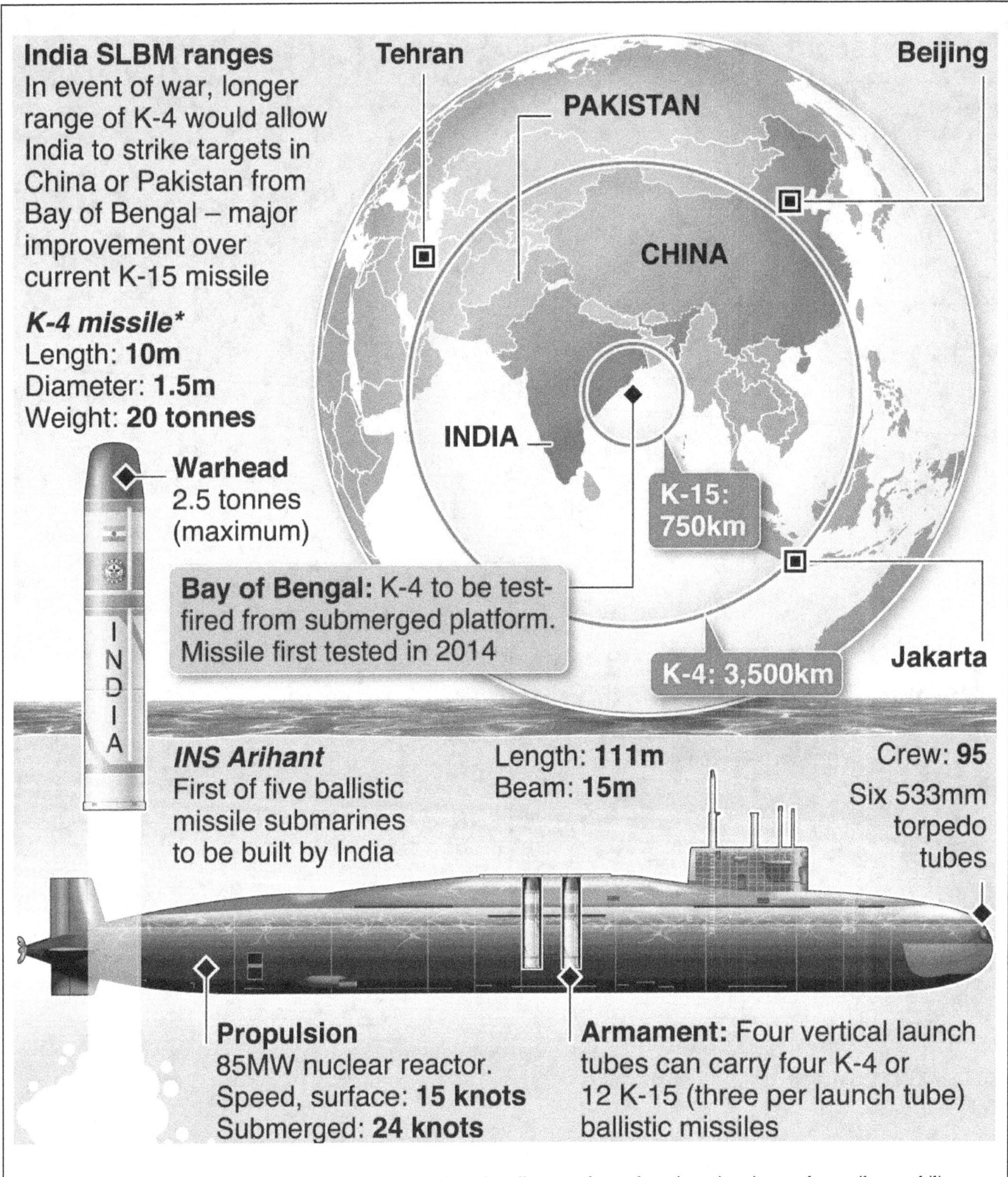

India's K-4 submarine launched ballistic missile (SLBM) from it Arihant nuclear submarine, gives it a nuclear strike capability against both China and Pakistan[291]

---

[291] Graphic news - https://www.graphicnews.com/en/pages/35130/MILITARY-India-K-4-nuclear-missile?var=d

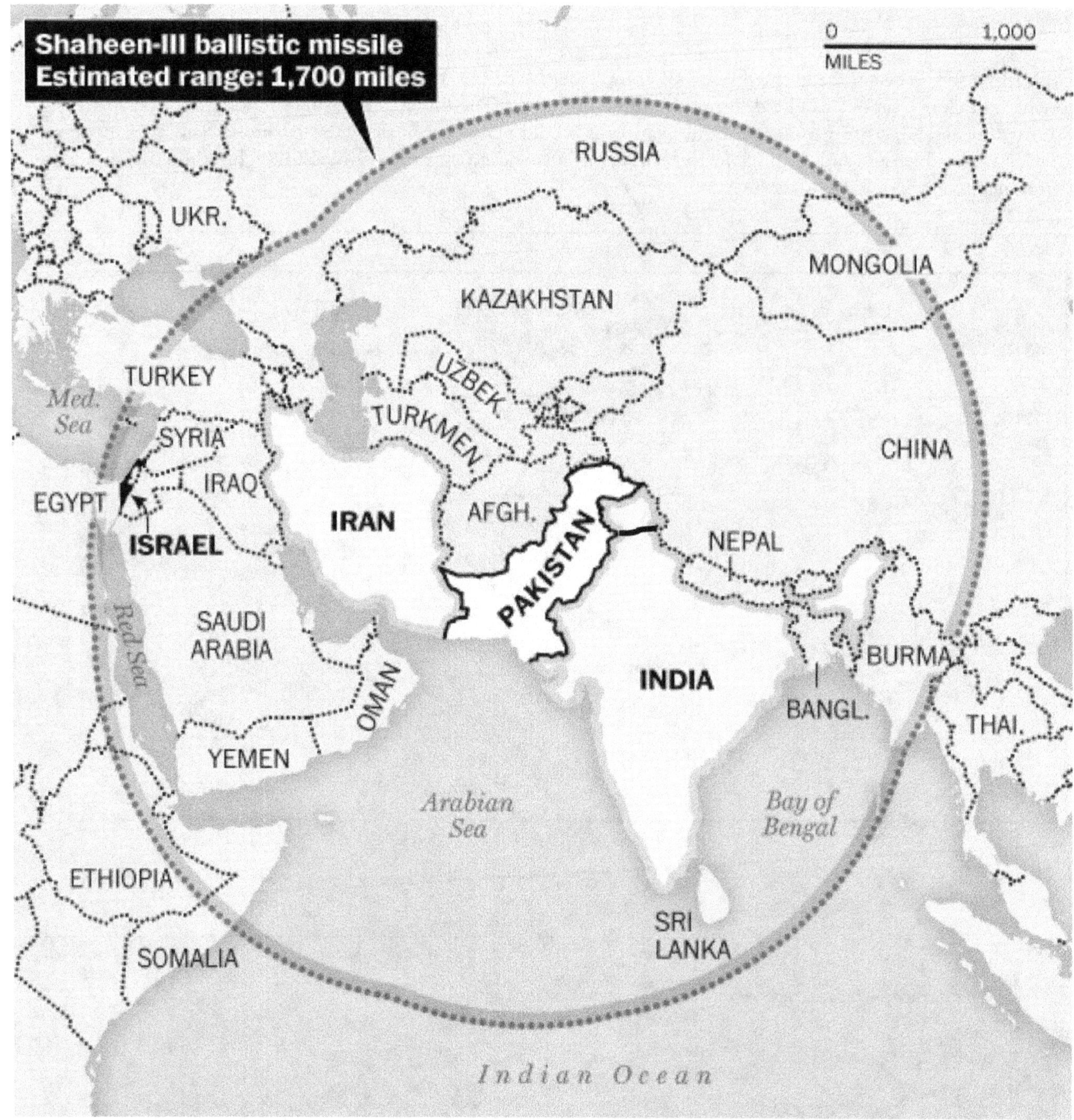

The Washington Post[292]

---

[292] https://www.washingtonpost.com/

Both India and Pakistan are in the process of completing a TRIAD (three-sided military-force structure) system – in which nuclear weapons can be delivered by air, land and sea. The theory underlying the triad was that spreading the nuclear assets across various weapons platforms would make the nuclear arsenal more likely to survive an attack by an adversary and to be able to respond to a nuclear first strike successfully.This should give added deterrence to any would be adversary.

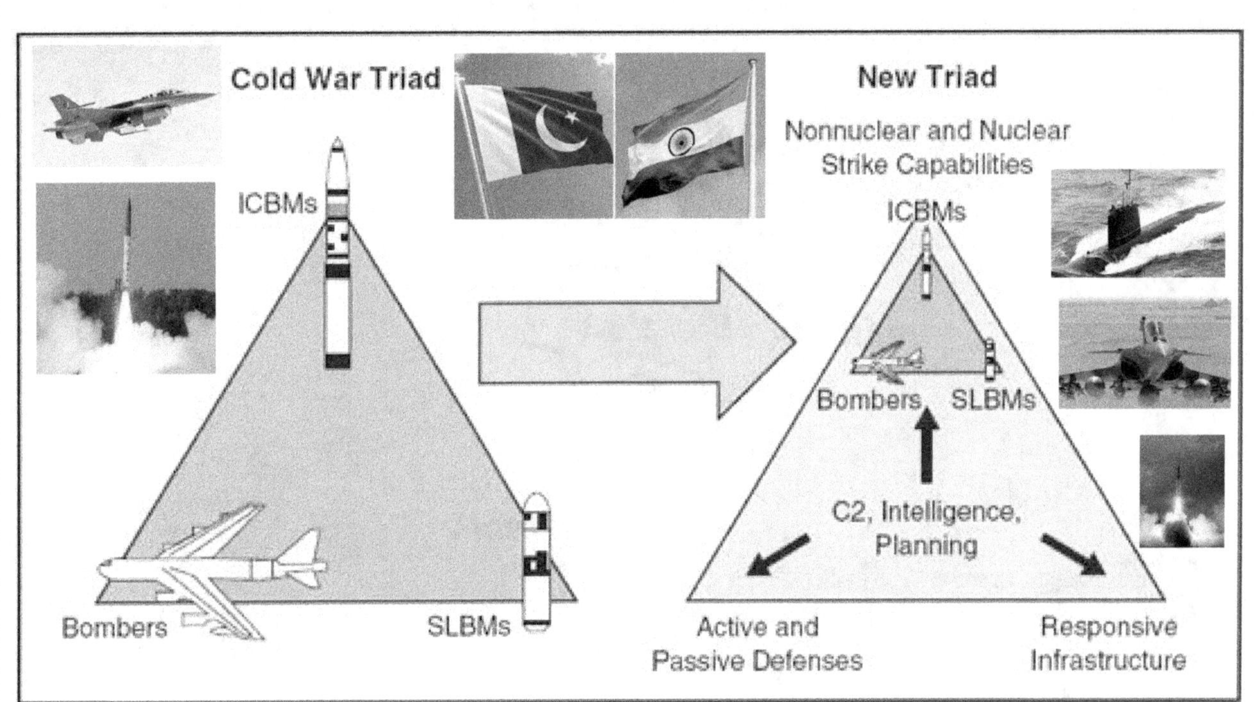

Pakistan, India in a naval and nuclear arms race - https://www.nextbigfuture.com/2015/10/700-nuclear-engineers-in-china-made.html

Pakistan's Nasr nuclear capable battlefield missile and french Rafael multirole combat aircraft (ordered by India)

Indian BMD will offer false sense of security

capability of intercepting a missile in the terminal phase.

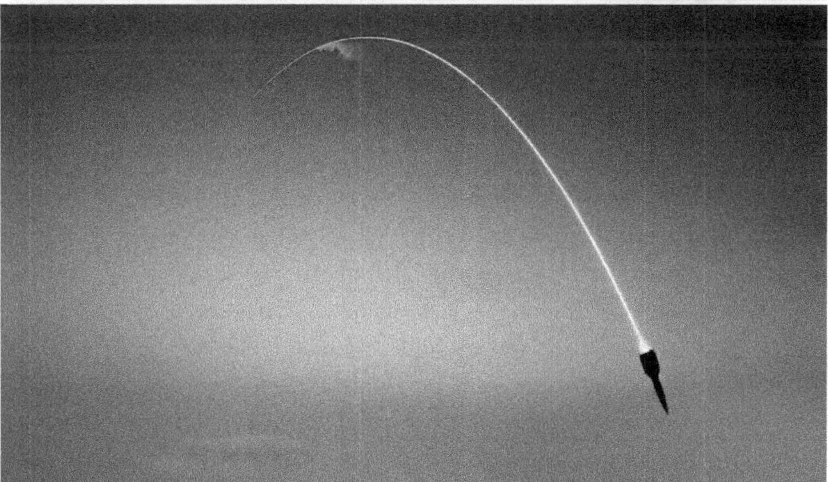

India has been working on a Ballistic missile Defence (BMD) shield to deter Pakistani missiles since 1999. In May 2001, the former US president George W. Bush prompted the Indian prime minister Atal Behari Vajpayee to acquire a BMD system – with assistance from the US and its allies (possibly to contain the missile threat from China and Russia). The US is seeing India as its counterweight to a rising China.[293]

Currently the Indian BMD has the

India has also joined the select group of nations that have a BMD system (US, Russia, Israel and China).[294] India has successfully test fired the indigenous interceptor missile Advanced Area Defence (AAD). Prime Minister Modi has said, **"with this India has demonstrated its ballistic missile defence capability"**.

The BMD provides a two-layered shield – it provides protection both against ballistic missiles that are outside (exo) as well as inside (endo) the earth's atmosphere. The system India is developing is capable of intercepting and destroying incoming targets at an altitude of 15 to 25 kms.

The interceptor is a single stage solid rocket-propelled guided missile, equipped with sophisticated state-of-the-art technology. It is thought that the interceptor missile has its own mobile launcher, secure data link for interception, independent tracking and homing capabilities and sophisticated radars. On 11 February 2017, a test was conducted in which the interceptor destroyed an incoming Prithvi missile. The incoming hostile ballistic missile target was successfully intercepted at a

---

293 Hasan Ehtisham, Indian BMD will offer false sense of security (2017) - https://tribune.com.pk/story/1503613/indian-bmd-will-offer-false-sense-security/

294 India's impregnable ballistic missile defence interceptor shield is a strong message to Pakistan - http://www.financialexpress.com/india-news/indias-impregnable-ballistic-missile-defence-interceptor-shield-is-a-strong-message-to-pakistan/572233/

high altitude (50 km). [295]

Kings College University professor Harsh V. Pant states, **"The Indian BMD will fuel instability and affect bilateral relations between India and Pakistan, which might further lower the nuclear threshold and tempt Pakistan to go for a nuclear first strike".** [296]

According to the analysts Hasan Ehtisham, **"Indian BMD will offer false sense of security….. BMD capability will give India a false sense of security and will push India to go for a first nuclear strike. Thus, it could seriously undermine the deterrence stability in South Asia…...The proficiency of the Indian BMD system is exceedingly debatable with respect to the geographical contiguity of India with Pakistan and China. During the Cold War, the distance between the US and the Soviet Union provided a necessary time for anti-ballistic missile (ABM) system to intercept an incoming missile. In case of India and Pakistan, the time gap is relatively too short to entirely attain necessary reconnaissance to efficiently intercept an incoming missile".** [297]

India's advance BMD missiles - Ashvin Advanced Defense (AAD) had successfully hit the incoming ballistic missile Dhanush, which was launched from Indian Navy vessel from the Bay of Bengal on the 15 May 2016 . It is argued that the primary reason for this test is to defend against any Pakistani ballistic missiles in the event of a conflict. It will also help India's Cold start doctrine of fighting a limited war with Pakistan under the shield of the BMD system. [298] India is also developing sophisticated technologies, such as nuclear submarines, SLBMs, Anti-satellite technologies (ASAT), cyber warfare technologies and shaping a Cold Start Doctrine (CSD) for a limited war. These technologies will impact on the stability and security of the regions deterrence.

According to the analyst Muhammad Suleman, **"The BMD system alone will severely undermine the strategic stability between these two relatively equivalent nuclear weapons states. It will not only disturb deterrence stability by limiting the enemy's capability to inflict 'unacceptable' damage, even if it can absorb a 'first strike', but it also instigates an opponent to strike first, if they believes they are threatened. Such developments increase the level of strategic instability so much that any false alarm, technical fault or miscalculation has the potential to become an accidental cause of war…..In times of crises, these technologies will cultivate a sense of military 'superiority 'in India, encouraging it to activate its provocative CSD strategy, under the cover of the ballistic missile shield and second strike capability".** [299]

In view of the BMD and other sophisticated technologies that India is developing, Pakistan has begun to counter these measures by developing its own range of technologies to ensure that deterrence is maintained within the region. Pakistan. It has increased its ballistic missiles, nuclear weapons stockpiles, in the process of completing its TRIAD system (Aircraft, ballistic missiles, Submarine Launched Cruise Missiles). It has successfully tested the Ababeel multiple independently targetable reentry vehicles Vehicles (MIRVs) missile, has made improvement in tactical missiles and this has assured second strike capability. Pakistan has developed the Ababeel surface-to-surface medium-range ballistic missile, with a maximum range of 2,200 kilometres (1,400 miles). The missile was tested on 24 January 2017 and demonstrates the level of Pakistan's sophistication in addressing its security needs. The missile has the ability to carry either conventional or nuclear warheads, and is claimed to use multiple independently targetable re-entry vehicles (MIRV). This would enable the Ababeel MIRVed missile to overwhelm any BDM defences that India could

---

[295] India's impregnable ballistic missile defence interceptor shield is a strong message to Pakistan - http://www.financialexpress.com/india-news/indias-impregnable-ballistic-missile-defence-interceptor-shield-is-a-strong-message-to-pakistan/572233/

[296] Ibid

[297] Hasan Ehtisham, Indian BMD will offer false sense of security (2017) - https://tribune.com.pk/story/1503613/indian-bmd-will-offer-false-sense-security/

[298] Muhammad Suleman, India's BMD System and Challenge to Strategic Stability - http://cpakgulf.org/2016/07/22/indias-bmd-system-and-challenge-to-strategic-stability/

[299] Ibid

put up, thus enhancing its second strike capability and deterrence.[300]

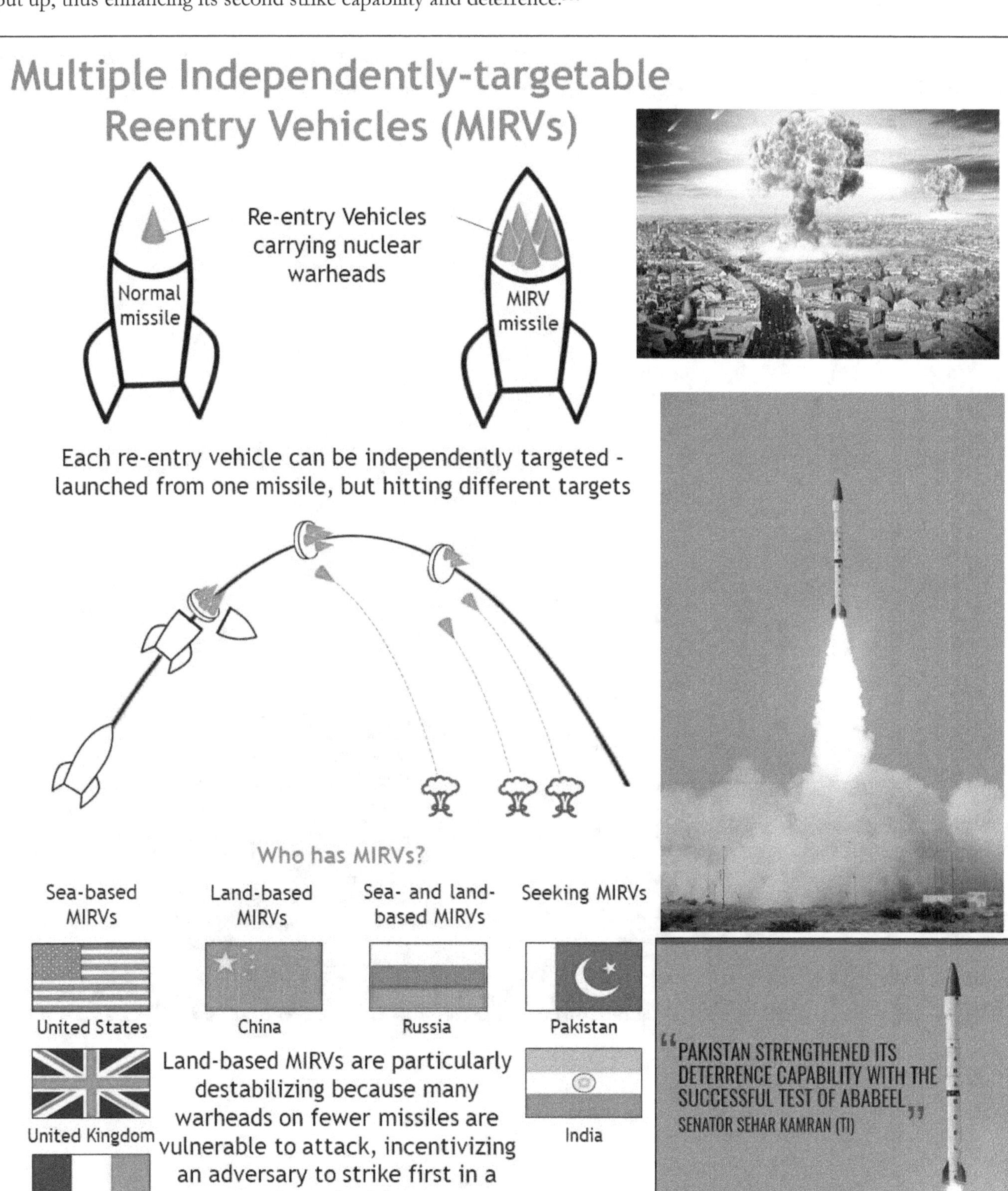

Currently 5 countries have known MIRV capability with Pakistan test's of the Ababeel missile making it the sixth

---

[300] Muhammad Suleman, India's BMD System and Challenge to Strategic Stability - http://cpakgulf.org/2016/07/22/indias-bmd-system-and-challenge-to-strategic-stability/

nation in the world to possess this capability. It is thought that India will also follow and suit and develop its own MIRV capability. The use of MIRVs on submarines is considered less destabilizing than on land-based missiles because the difficulty of finding nuclear submarines makes strikes against them unlikely. In January 2017 Pakistan tested a MIRVed missile (Ababeel). Senior Indian defense officials have indicated that India's Agni-class of missiles will eventually have MIRVed capability.issiles will be MIRVed.[301]

Image/pixabay.com/Patriot missile defence

---

[301] Multiple Independently-targetable Reentry Vehicle (MIRV) - https://armscontrolcenter.org/multiple-independently-targetable-reentry-vehicle-mirv/

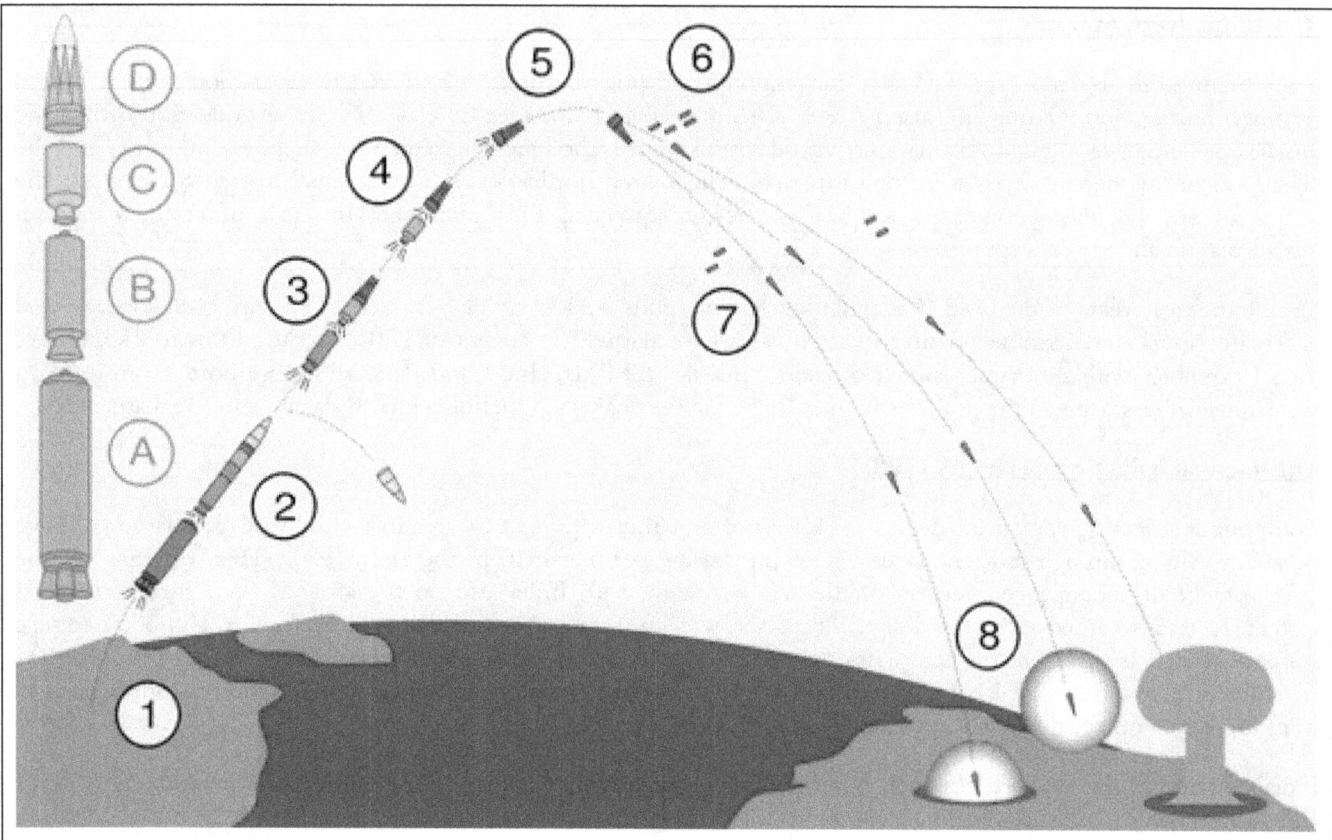

The above diagram showing the different stages of a MIRVed ICBM – in this case the US Minuteman III ballistic Missile.[302] The following sequences are given:

1. The missile launches out of its silo by firing its 1st stage boost motor (A).
2. About 60 seconds after launch, the 1st stage drops off and the 2nd stage motor (B) ignites. The missile shroud is ejected.
3. About 120 seconds after launch, the 3rd stage motor (C) ignites and separates from the 2nd stage.
4. About 180 seconds after launch, 3rd stage thrust terminates and the Post-Boost Vehicle (D) separates from the rocket.
5. The Post-Boost Vehicle maneuvers itself and prepares for re-entry vehicle (RV) deployment.
6. The RVs, as well as decoys and chaff, are deployed during backaway.
7. The RVs and chaff re-enter the atmosphere at high speeds and are armed in flight.
8. The nuclear warheads detonate, either as air bursts or ground bursts.

The significance of MIRV missile for Pakistan is that it becomes a force multiplier by delivering many warheads via one missile. It gives Pakistan the ability to strike multiple targets with a high level of precision and will disrupt or destroy the defensive capabilities of its adversary (radars and other sophisticated defence technolgies that woul aid an adversarys BMD capability). As technologies emerge further in the subcontinent, the costly arms race could lead to a nuclear nightmare if confidence building measures are not introduced by India and Pakistan. In conjuction with other nuclear powers, a serious attempt in reducing weapons of mass destruction and related technologies should be implemented to make the world a safer place for its inhabitants.[303]

---

[302] ICBM diagram - https://en.wikipedia.org/wiki/Wikipedia:Featured_picture_candidates/ICBM_diagram
[303] Pakistan's Ababeel ballistic missile ensures strategic stability in South Asia - https://www.globalvillagespace.com/pakistans-progression-in-ballistic-missiles-will-it-neutralize-india-or-bring-another-wave-of-arm-race/

Risk of inadvertent war?

Undermining the apparent 'stability' that conventional and nuclear forces have given to the region is their shared common border, and the ongoing dispute over Kashmir, which both sides lay claim to. The introduction of ballistic missiles has only exacerbated this insecurity. Add to this the psychological ingredient of nuclear superiority, and the likelihood of incoherent decision-making increases. The shared border leaves a very small margin for error at the outset of any hostilities compared to that of the superpowers, thus increasing the risk of conflict through miscalculation and misconception.[304]

During the early years of the Cold War, when nuclear weapons could only be delivered by aircraft, both superpowers had many hours to determine whether an alert was a false alarm. The advent of ICBMs reduced this to 25 minutes, then 10 minutes with submarine-launched ballistic missiles (SLBMs). India and Pakistan's close borders produce an almost negligible warning time of three minutes, reducing the chances of defining a false alarm from a real attack.[305]

Anti-tactical ballistic missiles (ATBMs)

Compounding Pakistan's concern were credible reports of India's pursuit of an anti-tactical ballistic missile (ATBM) capability, either through indigenous design or purchasing off-the-shelf, in the early 1990s. This was through the development of an improved version of the Akash system, with India also on the lookout for a more advanced system. It has also asked Israel for designs of its Arrow ATBM, whilst negotiating with Russia for its S-300V missile systems (touted as similar to the U.S. Patriot system). The acquisition of an advanced air defence system with ATBM capability will give India the capability to intercept tactical ballistic missiles with ranges of over 300km. India claims to want these systems for the defence of New Delhi and Bombay.[306]

India's interest in missile defences appears to be driven primarily by Pakistan's acquisition and development of M-11 and Hatf series of ballistic missiles in the early 1990s. Pakistani defence officials have acknowledged that Pakistan would find such as development threatening and could respond by increasing its nuclear and missile capabilities.

Strategic Implications of an Indian Missile Defence System

A sophisticated Indian air defence system with ATBM capabilities could seriously undermine Pakistan's reliance on the M-11/Ghauri ballistic missile and on its tactical strike aircraft (e.g, F-16, JF-17 and reconditioned Mirage III) as its primary nuclear- capable delivery systems. India has also modernised its air defences with the purchase and license production of Russian-made Su-30MKI fighter-bombers and the Tunguska low-altitude air defence system.[307]

Moreover, its planned acquisition of French Mirage 2000 fighters has been held up by financial and political problems. Pakistan's missile programmes are driven by a desire to augment limited offensive air capabilities against India (which holds a nearly 2:1 advantage in combat aircraft) and to field a more effective delivery system. Therefore, without a credible aerial delivery capability, Pakistan will have to rely mainly on ballistic missiles to overwhelm India's defences. Unable to match India's defensive systems, Pakistan's initial response could entail increasing the number of nuclear weapons and delivery systems available at short notice, in order to restore its deterrent.[308]

India's acquisition of an ATBM could therefore destabilise the existing nuclear balance by depriving Pakistan of an assured strike capability, thus allowing India to engage in a conventional war, or invade Pakistan-held Kashmir, without fear of nuclear retaliation. Given the large imbalance of conventional forces between India and Pakistan, the outcome of such a conflict is not in doubt. The danger lies in a sharp reaction to any perceived 'ill-intended' exercise, such as the 'brass-tack' military exercise by India in 1987, which heightened tensions between the two countries.[309]

Pakistan's options would be either to match India's defences, or overwhelm India's capability. Its short-term

---

[304] Zian Mian, No time to think, Jang Publishers Ltd, 1998, Pg10

[305] Ibid

[306] Afzal Mahmood, Mini-Starwars in Asia? Dawn Publishers Ltd, 1999, Pg1

[307] Ibid

[308] Ibid

[309] Ibid

prospects for either are slim, due in part to its own economic conditions and also to the punitive sanctions imposed on both states by the West after the 1998 nuclear tests. The United States is currently barred from supplying Pakistan with any military equipment due to the Pressler Amendment, and Russia's close relations with India make major arms sales to Pakistan unlikely. Pakistan's long-term prospects of acquiring a missile defence system are greater through China, which has renewed its close relationship with Pakistan after India's nuclear tests. China is believed to be working on its own ATBM capability.[310]

Pakistan- notwithstanding its smaller defence budget and resources base-is capable of building up its nuclear offensive deterrent incrementally. This could entail increasing the number of nuclear weapons available for both missile and aircraft delivery, acquiring cruise missiles, and developing decoys and penetration aids to saturate India's active defences. The introduction of an ostensibly defensive ATBM capability into by India has increased the potential of a full-fledged, South Asian nuclear arms race.[311]

Pakistan's Shaheen-III medium-range ballistic missile (MRBM) is carried by a 16-wheel transporter erector launcher (TEL)

---

[310] Mahmood, op cit:3
[311] Ibid

Chapter 8: Arms Control and Confidence-Building-Measures

Arms Control and Confidence-Building Measures

The nuclear tests in 1998 have established a form of defence equilibrium. The consequences of a nuclear conflict would be enormously destructive, with neither side being a winner. There is a real concern that the long-standing hostility between India and Pakistan could overwhelm any deterrent advantage gained from these weapons. The need for continued, relentless dialogue is all too apparent given the short history of both nations.

Over the years Pakistan has proposed numerous bilateral nuclear arms control initiatives with India, declaring, for example, that it would be prepared to join the NPT or accept other non-proliferation measures if India did so. India has rejected these proposals, arguing that they do not address the nuclear threat India faces from China and that nuclear disarmament questions should be addressed as a global, rather than as a regional issue. Pakistan and India have, however adopted a number of bilateral confidence-building measures, including a military-to-military hot-line and an agreement, which entered into force in January 1991, prohibiting the two states from attacking each other's nuclear installations. Lists of facilities covered by this agreement are now also exchanged periodically.[312]

<u>Actual measures Pakistan and India could take</u>

Tackle the Kashmir Problem Positively.

It is obvious that nuclear risk reduction will not get anywhere if there is no movement towards a broader settlement on Kashmir. Pending a solution to the dispute, progress is essential in dealing with the immediate sources of tension to build a climate of normalcy and pave the way to a just Kashmir settlement.

The two nations should attempt to humanise the problem of Kashmir, rather than engage in political and military tit-

---

[312] Ashok Kapur, Pakistan's attitude to the NPT, Parchment Press, 1993, Pg25

for-tat. The alleviation of human suffering in Kashmir should be the overriding concern of both sides. Confidence building measures could include the safeguarding of fundamental human rights, unconditional release of Kashmiri prisoners, unifying divided families, providing access to international humanitarian organisations in occupied Kashmir and granting Kashmiri's the right to a fair trial. This is by no means an exhaustive list, but illustrative of how to humanise the problem in order to deal with its most urgent dimensions.[313]

Limitations placed on missile deployments and warheads.

Limitations on offensive weapon systems, curtailment of forward build-up of military cantonments and airfields would be a positive gesture for peace. None of these measures would deprive India or Pakistan of deterrence or defence capability. While Pakistan has around 8 or so forward airfields, India has over 15 forward and 16 medium-range airfields. Apart from these, it has only 9-10 remaining military fields in the rear. Given the range of India's military aircraft and its Prithvi missiles, closing some of these forward airfields would restore confidence on both sides.[314] Secondly, an overt nuclear deterrence will now allow Pakistan to cut down on conventional defence spending – this is of vital interest to Pakistan. A beginning can be made on a treaty similar to the Conventional Forces in Europe Treaty. The logic of that treaty is equally applicable here, i.e. to reduce the chances of surprise attacks and stabilise the military balance, rather than eliminating military forces per se from the region.[315]

Reduce the number of Soldiers and their main equipment deployed along the borders.

Both sides should focus on limitations on the number of troops, armoured and mechanised formations from each other's borders, eventually leading to the reduction of conventional offensive capabilities. India's rationale of the threats from other neighbours like China or even Bangladesh does not hold within this context, since the armoured and mechanised formations are really only suitable, terrain-wise, against Pakistan. Also a mutual agreement not to deploy armoured divisions in areas where surprise attack is possible, specifically in the central and desert plateau along the Indo-Pakistan border. That whole area can be declared a tank-free zone.

A reduction in new weapon systems.

A move towards prohibiting the induction of the latest technologies and weapons into their conventional forces would also be welcome. The underlying mutual minimal nuclear deterrence would lessen the need for the importance of 'state-of-the-art' weapons technologies. Defence acquisitions of new weapon systems and new technology should be made the subject of mutual discussions. For this reason, any nuclear risk reduction objective requires addressing the conventional asymmetry between Pakistan and India to reduce Pakistan's greater need for missiles. These are already regarded as both feasible and cost-effective by its defence planners.

Increase nuclear co-operation between each other.

The eventual recognition and acceptance of each other's nuclear weapons capability can lead to co-operation, if desired, especially in terms of multilateral nuclear fuel centres, where technology can be jointly controlled. Given the problem both countries face in terms of conventional power generation, including the costs, nuclear power can become a viable alternative. Here the security route can eventually lead to direct economic benefits.[316]

India and Pakistan should sign a Non-Aggression Pact.

Pakistan must move towards evolving a non-aggression pact – either at the bilateral level or the South Asian nations multilateral level. Such a pact differs from a no-war pact and does not deny the use of the military option in self-defence – it only denies parties the option of aggressing against other parties to the pact. It calls on both sides to commit to agreements not to aggress against each other within a military framework. This implies that both India and Pakistan cannot simply intensify exchanges along the line of control (LoC) into an all-our war against their international borders. A non-aggression pact will further build on the confidence-and security-building measures (CSBMs) involving the hot-line, communication facilities between commanders on both sides of the LoC and other

---

[313] Maleeha Lodhi, Nuclear Risk reduction and Conflict-Resolution in South Asia, Jang Publications Ltd, 1998, Pg11
[314] Ibid
[315] Ibid
[316] Ibid

such measures – some of which are already in place but not adhered to strictly.[317]

Sign the major International Treaties.

Along with a proposal for a non-aggression pact, Pakistan must go a step further in its moves towards joining the mainstream nuclear powers by agreeing to sign the **CTBT** as a nuclear weapon state. Already Pakistan has made one wise move in this field by declaring its intentions of not exporting its nuclear technology.

The Comprehensive Test Ban Treaty (CTBT) - Pakistan has sensibly delinked the issue of its signing the CTBT from what India does. The reason for this is simple – neither India nor Pakistan can conduct anymore nuclear tests underground – at least in the foreseeable future. So there is no need for Pakistan to hold out on the CTBT. As for the CTBT itself, it deals specifically with nuclear tests which it seeks to prohibit completely. Its verification and on – site clauses also deal with test sites and not with reactors and other weapons – producing installations.[318]

The Non-Proliferation Treaty (NPT) - Pakistan has been under considerable pressure for a number of years to unconditionally sign the NPT. India carried out nuclear tests in 1974 and has not signed the NPT. Pakistan has insisted that it will not sign the treaty until India has also done so.[319]

Missile Technology Control Regime (MTCR) - With the successful testing of the Ghauri and Agni missiles, Pakistan and India can both become party to the MTCR. This would allay fears that Pakistan would supply missile technology to other Muslim states. The MTCR is basically a suppliers club and places no restrictions on member states developing their own missile systems.[320]

All the above measures deal with reality of the Pakistan-India situation on the ground - with neither state having to renounce its defence capability even as mutual deterrence it strengthened. Until such times as the conflicts are resolved at least the two states will be refraining themselves from unrestrained and destabilising arms races - and will have moved from a cold war style, unstable relationship to a more stable, détente framework of interaction.

The goal of international efforts should now progressively turn to preventing further nuclear tests, persuading India and Pakistan to halt the production of fissile materials for nuclear explosives and taking other steps to head off a South Asian nuclear Arms Race, such as pressing both sides to curb their ballistic missile programmes.

Pakistan former Army chief greeting servicemen and PAF JF-17 Thunder multi-role combat aircraft.

---

[317] Ibid
[318] Lodhi, op cit:12
[319] Ibid
[320] Ibid

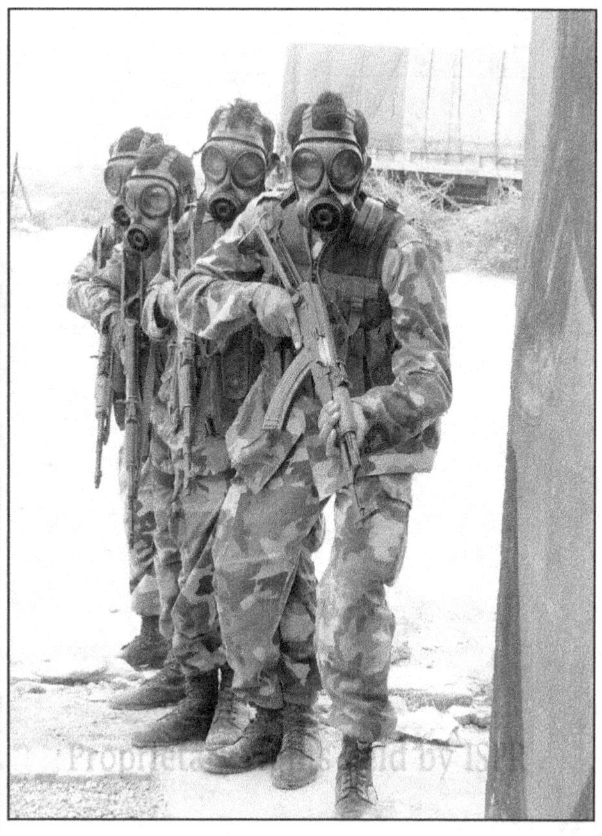

(above) Pakistani Special Services Group (SSG)[321]

(Left) Indian troops on parade

---

[321] Special Services Group (SSG) - https://www.pakistanarmy.gov.pk/AWPReview/ImageEnlarged.aspx?GalleryID=26&ImageID=399

Peace: Confidence-building measures, such as the recent meeting between Pakistan Army DGMO Maj. Gen. Aamer Riaz (right) and his Indian counterpart Lt. Gen. Vinod Bhatia (left) at the Wagah Border, are vital to the country's political future[322]

---

[322] This year, India must keep violence out of politics - http://www.dailymail.co.uk/indiahome/indianews/article-2532916/This-year-India-violence-politics.html

Indian and Pakistani troops – confidence building measures

Peace between India and Pakistan should be a must for their foreign policy priority

Chapter 9: Conclusion

CONCLUSION

The main threat to the region is the dispute over the state of Kashmir. The uprising in Indian occupied Kashmir could spiral out of control and lead both nuclear powers to a catastrophic nuclear war. The consequences of this potential nuclear war, will not just be on the death and destruction in India and Pakistan, but it will also have global ramifications. Pakistan's main threat perceptions emanate from India. Its main concerns include India's military build-up, both conventionally and nuclear, and its ability to deliver nuclear payloads due to its ever-increasing ballistic capabilities (including the Prithvi and Agni surface-to-surface missiles and nuclear capable IAF fighters). India now has the nuclear command-and-control centres required to integrate nuclear weapons and related assets. Its Akash anti-missile missile, claimed to be superior to the US Patriot, is also being positioned to intercept incoming Ghauri and Hatf missiles, which has created another security headache for Pakistan's defence planners.[323]

India's assertive posture since the 1971 war has increased in the last few years, particularly following the advent of the BJP fundamentalist government. Although the BJP government has attempted to explain that India's military build-up is defensive and commensurate with India's overall economic growth, others in the region cannot be so sure of India's intentions.[324]

The area of concern for Western security analysts is the absence of proper command and control over the sub-continent nuclear arms race. Without the appropriate checks and balances, the 1.35 billion people of South Asia are vulnerable to a potential nuclear war between India and Pakistan. This grim prospect is enhanced given the intensity of distrust and active hostility over Kashmir. Any cross-border nuclear attack will arrive without sufficient warning for

---

[323] News International, Armed to the Teeth, Jang Publishers Ltd, 1998, Pg10
[324] Johann Mcgeary, India's Surprise Nuclear Tests, The Time, May 25, 1998, Pg34

both sides, as the flight time of Prithvi or Ghauri missiles will be under three minutes, giving insufficient time for evacuation contingency or retaliatory response. The prospect of an unstable regime getting into power is also very high on both sides. The ethnic unrest that is characteristic of the Indian sub-continent also highlights the dangers of a terrorist or dictatorial regime having access to weapons of mass destruction.[325]

Furthermore, the hostility of South Asian countries has contributed to the massive arms build-up in the region. The threat perceptions (primarily the Kashmir dispute) in this region has led these countries to purchase 'state-of-the-heart' sophisticated arms, this has resulted in altering the security of each country in the region. There is an urgent need that better sense prevails in New Delhi and nuclear militarisation is stopped. Pakistan's defence policy is basically reactive to Delhi's defence agenda. Nonetheless, there is an urgent need for confidence building measures to be positively integrated into both nations' foreign policies to ease tensions, and also for a focus on the real issues of poverty and illiteracy, instead of concentrating on tit-for-tat responses to each nation's rhetoric.

However, tensions exist primarily with India and Pakistan and the future looks bleak, with numerous occasions where war has been imminent, usually over Kashmir. With the advanced military equipment incorporated into their respective armies and the acquisition of weapons of mass destruction (especially their nuclear capability), there is a serious risk of a nuclear war occurring between these two neighbours in the very near future. India and Pakistan need to draw the lessons for the horrific outcome of the two Japanese cities that were destroyed by the American nuclear bombs (Hiroshima and Nagasaki). A nuclear war is not an option, and the sabre rattling between these two countries need to stop. India has to stop its oppressive tactics in Indian occupied Kashmir, it should not think that its economic might will hide the atrocities that have been attributed to the over 700,000 troops that are carrying out suppressive operations in Kashmir.

The World should also try to help and resolve this issue, a plebiscite should resolve this long simmering dispute. Indian claim of being the largest democracy does not go well in the Kashmir region, where Indian troops brutal tactics have further alienated the people. There is widespread evidence of genocide being committed by Indian security forces and the world needs to put pressure on India and make it accountable to the evidence of widespread atrocities in Kashmir. Both India and Pakistan need to resolve this conflict on an amicable basis, and help develop both countries on an economic basis and improve the welfare of its citizens – otherwise the dispute over Kashmir has the potential to spiral out of control and lead to a full scale nuclear war. The Kashmir issue is the world's most dangerous flashpoint that has the highest chance of a nuclear war occurring – it is deemed by many to be more serious that the Cuban Missile Crisis and North Korea's nuclear sabre rattling.

Pakistani Army Strategic Arsenal (nuclear capable ballistic missile)

---

[325] Zakaria, op cit:26

References

Afzal Mahmood, Mini-Starwars in Asia?, Dawn publishers Ltd, 1998

Anthony H.Cordesman, Western Strategic Interests and the India-Pakistan Military Balance, Ian Allan Ltd, 1988

Arnett, Nuclear stability and arms sales to India, Arms Control Today, 1997

Ashok Kapur, Pakistan's attitude to the NPT, Parchment Press, 1993

B.H.Farmer, An Introduction to South Asia, Richard Clay & Co.Ltd, 1983

Brassey's, World Aircraft & Systems Directory, Brassey's Ltd, 1996

C. Philips, The nuclear Casebook, Polygon Books, 1983

Chapter Six: Asia, 2018, The Military Balance, vol. 118, no. 1, pp. 219

Chapter six: Asia. (2017). *The Military Balance, 117*(1), 237-350.

Chris Bishop, Encyclopedia of Air Warfare-Volume 2, Aerospace Publishing Ltd, 1997

Chris Taylor, Military Balance in Southeast Asia, House of Commons Library, 2011

Christopher Walker and Michael Evans, Pakistan Feared Israeli Raid, The Times, Wednesday June 3, 1998

Christopher Walker, Israel's Helped India for 20 years, The Times, Thursday June 4, 1998

Cindy Shiner, International Herald Tribune, 1998

David Albright and Tom Zamora, India and Pakistan go Nuclear, Bulletin of Atomic Scientists, 1989

Dawn Weekly, Kashmir Policy, Touch Media Co.Ltd, 1998

Defence.pk - https://defence.pk/

Edward W.Desmond, Unity or Chaos?, Time, November 12, 1990

Eric Arnett, Delhi able to play nuclear trump in game for control of Kashmir, The Times, May 1998

Eric Arnett, Military Capacity and the Risk of War-China, India, Pakistan and Iran, Oxford University Press, 1997

Eric Arnett, What Threat?, Bulletin of the Atomic Scientists, 1997

Fareed Zakaria, How to be a Great Cheap, NewsWeek, T.P.L Printers Ltd, May 25, 1998

Flickr - https://www.flickr.com/search/?text=jf-17%20thunder

Flight International, Airforces of the World Directory, Marketforce Ltd, 1998

General Walter Walker, The Next Domino?, The Covenant Publishing Co.Ltd, 1980

Global Security - https://www.globalsecurity.org/

Government of Pakistan, Ministry of Defence - http://www.mod.gov.pk/

Hafeez Malik, Dilemmas of National Security and Co-operation, The Macmillan Press Ltd, 1993

Ibid

IISS, Strategic Survey 2011 – The Annual Review of World Affairs, Routledge, 2011

IISS, Strategic Survey 2012 – The Annual Review of World Affairs, Routledge, 2012

IISS, Strategic Survey 2013 – The Annual Review of World Affairs, Routledge, 2013

Impact International, Delhi Expands its Strategic Swath, News & Media Ltd, 1996

Imtiaz Bakhari, The beginning of another 'Great Game'?, Jang Publishers Ltd, September 26, 1998

Indian Air Force - http://indianairforce.nic.in/

Indian Navy - https://www.indiannavy.nic.in/

Indian Army - https://indianarmy.nic.in/index.aspx

India Today, Future Fire, 1998

India Today, Games of Brinkmanship, 1987

India Today, India and Pakistan hours away from a nuclear war, 1994

India Today, India is now a nuclear weapon state, Living India Media Ltd, May 1998

India Today, India is now a Nuclear Weapon State, Living Media India Ltd, 1998

India Today, Pakistan's nuclear test, what now, June 1998

Inter Services Public Relations (ISPR) - https://www.ispr.gov.pk/

International Institute for Strategic Studies (IISS), Military Balance 1998-99, Oxford University Press, 1998

J.A.S Greenville, History of the World, HarperCollins Publishers, 1994

J.Goldstein & J. Pevehouse, International Relations, United States, 2007

Jane Nolan, Ballistic Missiles in the Third World, Brookings Institutions, 1991

Janes 360 - http://www.janes.com/article/search?query=+JF-17

Janes Defence Weekly (JDW), On the Line of Fire, Janes Information Group Ltd, 1998

JDW, A Loss of Momentum, 1997

JDW, A Loss of Momentum, 1997

JDW, Asia's Missile Race Hots Up, 1994

JDW, Asia's Missile Race Hots Up, 1994

JDW, Country Survey- Pakistan, 1992

JDW, Country Survey-India, 1990

JDW, Country Survey-Pakistan, 1992

JDW, Fighting on the Roof of the World, 1998

JDW, IAF Follows up on Su-30 Offer, 1994

JDW, India and Pakistan move to prevent nuclear disaster, March 1999

JDW, India becomes Sixth Nuclear Weapons State, 1998

JDW, India Budget May Affect Modernisation, 1998

JDW, India's Search for a New SPG, 1994

JDW, Indian Budget Fall May Affect Modernisation, 1998

JDW, Latest Tests put India in Nuclear Arms Spotlight, 1998

JDW, Mounting Tensions in South Asia, 1996

JDW, Nuclear Submarine is being built in India, December 1994

JDW, Pakistan Needs up to 70 Nuclear Warheads, June 1998

JDW, Pakistan's Time for Reassessment, 1998

JDW, Trials Provide Data for Range of Weapons Yields, 1998

JDW, USA links Chinese ties to missile Exports, 1994

Johann Mcgeary, India's Surprise Nuclear Tests, Time May 25, 1998

Lawrence Freedman, Atlas of Global Strategy, Macmillan Press Ltd, 1985

Lawrence Freedman, National Pride sets the Sabre Rattling, Daily Mail, May 29, 1998

Mahnaz Ipahani, Pakistan: dimensions of insecurity, Brassey's, 1990

Maleeha Lodhi, Nuclear Risk reduction and Conflict-Resolution in South Asia, Jang Publications Ltd, 1998

Mark J. Valencia, Trouble Waters, The Bulletin of the Atomic Scientists, 1997

Mustaq Ali Khan, Pakistan Army Green Book, Ferozsons (Pvt) Ltd, 1990

News International, Advani's Nuclear Blackmail, August 10, 1998

News International, India will have to reclaim Azaad Kashmir says Defence Minister, Jang Publications Ltd, 1998

News International, Nuclear arms not to be used: Nawaz, June 1998

Nick Bisley, Building Asia's Security, Routledge, 2009

Nils Bhinda, The Kashmir Conflict-1990, Earthscan Publication Ltd, 1994

Official Gateway To The Government Of Pakistan - http://www.pakistan.gov.pk/index.html

Pakistan Air Force - http://www.paf.gov.pk/

Patrick Brogan, World Conflicts-Why and Where they are Happening, Bloomsbury Publishing Ltd, 1992

Paul Dibb, Towards a New Balance of Power in Asia, Adelphi Paper 295, Oxford University Press, 1995

Paul Rogers, Guide to Nuclear Weapons 1984-85, C.J.W Printers Ltd, 1984

Peter G. Tsourus, Changing Orders-The Evolution of the World's Armies, Arms and Armour Press, 1994

Pixabay
https://pixabay.com/en/photos/?q=military&image_type=&cat=&min_height=&min_width=&order=popular&pagi=2

Quwa Defence News & Analysis Group - https://quwa.org

Sean Kay, Global Security in the Twenty-First Century, Rowman & Littlefield Publishers, Inc, 2006

Sidney Bearman, Strategic Survey 1993-1994, Published by Brassey's for the IISS, 1994

Stockholm International Peace Research Institute (SIPRI), World Military Expenditure Prices 1987-96, Oxford University Press, 1997

Sunday Telegraph, India Celebrates its Nuclear dream, May 1998

Tarun Basu, Selective Satellite Tracking of Missiles Alledged, India Abroad, 1997

The Daily Telegraph, Nuclear Blasts Puts Pakistan in Arms Race, 1998

The Economist, Asian Security, Published by the Economist Newspaper Ltd, 1996

The Military Balance, 01/2017, Volume 117, Issue 1

The News International, Armed to the Teeth, Jang Publishers Ltd, 1998

The Times, Pakistan Blasts into the Arms Race, Times Newspaper Ltd, 1998

Umer Farooq, Striking Consequences, Janes Defence Weekly, 2 September 1998

Venon Hewit, The New International Politics of South Asia, Manchester University Press, 1997

Walter Walker, The Next Domino?, The Covenant Publishing Ltd, 1980

Y. Ammar, The Kashmir Factor, Palestine Times, 9 October 1991

Zian Mian, No time to think, Jang Publishers Ltd, 1998

INDEX

Images in this book fall under the following categories

(a) public domain (applicable to most official photos released by the military/maufacturers)
(b) free for commercial use
(c) used with explicit permission from the owner (applicable to all images from private websites)
(d) assumed to fall under (a) or (b) (applicable to images in printed media where no image owner is identified)

ABOUT THE AUTHOR

Saghir Iqbal is a researcher in International Relations and Security Studies. He is an experienced Intelligence Analyst and has achieved a number of qualifications in this field. He is also a Lecturer in Business Management as well as an Examiner for A Level History and Business. Saghir Iqbal has a subject specialism in the following areas:

International Politics of the Cold War 1945-1991
Conflict Resolution in International Society+
Global and North-South Security Studies
Britain in the World
Disarmament Processes: History and Theory
Nationalism and Ethnicity in Post-Cold War Politics
Middle East: Area in Conflict
European Security
International Politics of the Environment
The United Nations, Peacekeeping and Intervention
Disarmament Processes: Current Problems
Globalisation and the South
International Terrorism
International Politics and Security Studies
Introduction to Peace Studies
Politics of the Global Environment
Regional Security in East Asia
Critical Security studies

Recently released books (2018)

- Dangerous Flashpoints in East Asia: The Military Build-up
- JF-17 Thunder: The Making of a Modern Cost- effective Multi-role Combat Aircraft
- Pakistan's War Machine: An Encyclopedia of its Weapons, Strategy and Military Security

9 781717 040404